Responding to Anger

Responding to Anger

A Workbook

Lorrainne Bilodeau, M.S.

 HAZELDEN®

Hazelden
Center City, Minnesota 55012-0176

1-800-328-0094
1-651-213-4590 (Fax)
www.hazelden.org

Library of Congress Cataloging-in-Publication Data
Bilodeau, Lorrainne.
     Responding to anger: a workbook / Lorrainne Bilodeau.
       p. cm.
     Includes bibliographical references.
     ISBN 1-56838-624-9
     1. Anger. 2. Interpersonal conflict. I. Title.

BF575.A5 R47 2001
152.4'7—dc21
                                                           00-054059

Editor's note
All the stories in this book are based on actual experiences. The names and details
have been changed to protect the privacy of the people involved. In some cases,
composites have been created.

This guide is not meant to supplant professional counseling or therapy. If you have
destructive thoughts about yourself or someone else, seek professional advice.

05 04 03 02 01   6 5 4 3 2

Cover design by Theresa Gedig
Interior design by Elizabeth Cleveland
Typesetting by Stanton Publication Services, Inc.

To Russell, Aunt Grace, and Ray

Contents

Acknowledgments

THERE ARE PEOPLE WHO CONTRIBUTED directly to the creation of this informational manual by offering clinical advice and opinions. Others helped me maintain my sanity, physical health, and professional career through depletion of my mental energy and emotional reserves in order to bring about its completion. These generous human beings include but are not limited to:

Alida Mason, L.C.S.W., who contributed clinical insight about responding to infant anger, kept my ego in perspective with her distorted sense of humor and fed me excellent manicotti.

Torie Adelman, whose tolerance, encouragement, and ability to ignore my irritable nature kept me mentally and emotionally stable.

Dave Mason, L.P. His willingness to share clinical experiences, concepts, and language skills often kept my ideas moving and my fingers typing.

Missie Oxendine, who graciously taught me the more subtle nuances of adolescent behavior and who courageously tried my ideas on her teenage daughter.

Carol Hoffman, C.S.S., who helped gather research material and who provided entertaining conversation during espresso breaks.

The many teenagers passing through Bethesda Link, who so willingly and freely shared information about themselves and their perspectives on life.

Introduction

IN THE EARLY 1990s, I wrote *The Anger Workbook,* a collection of information and exercises to help people understand and express their anger productively. I hesitated to discuss responding to other people's anger in that workbook. I was afraid it would encourage readers to focus on other people's anger and neglect their own. At the same time, I realized that a work about anger cannot be complete without at least introducing the topic of effectively responding to another person's angry feelings. As a compromise between my fear and my need for thoroughness, I presented two exercises in the last chapter and a brief explanation of an effective method for responding to another's anger.

I now believe my fear was unfounded. The experience of responding effectively to another's anger is generated from the responder's needs and requires that individual to focus as much on self as on the other person. I came to this conclusion by listening to many different people.

A tax collector said, "If I could get beyond my clients' anger more quickly, I'm sure I could do my job more efficiently." A woman asked, "How can I talk to my husband when he is angry? I always freeze up. I don't know what to say, and then he gets angrier. And then we don't talk. And then I think that I'm failing as a wife." The father of a teenage boy said, "I want to be a good father, but my son's aggression overwhelms the family. Everyone's afraid of him. I don't know what to do." Many business managers are frustrated by their employees' anger. They say, "No matter what I try to do to respond to their angry complaints, it just isn't enough—

they find something else to complain about. Then they get the other workers complaining, and nothing gets done."

People want to perform their work, family, and social roles well because it makes their lives easier and enhances self-esteem. They want the skills to face another person's anger fearlessly, to defuse aggressive outbursts, and to use relational anger to build stronger, healthier relationships.

I began doing workshops designed to help people learn these skills. As the years went by, I would periodically run into people who had participated in them. They were always willing to share how the skills they learned gave them more confidence, reduced their anxiety, and helped them develop stronger relationships. The tax collector told me, "I probably do my job more efficiently and I definitely have less stress." The wife who spoke to me about her husband was able to step beyond the fear reaction to anger she had learned in childhood. This enabled her to tell her husband how his outbursts triggered deep responses for her. She opened the door for him to respond positively, and as their communication grew, their emotional intimacy grew.

The father whose family was being tyrannized by his adolescent's anger helped his wife learn and accept the benefits of natural consequences. Together, they were able to use these consequences to obtain help for their son.

Managers have returned to tell me that understanding the dynamics of anger gave them confidence when facing complaining employees. With their new self-assurance, they were able to defuse the anger, enhance morale, and increase productivity.

Obtaining results like those described above does not involve focusing on or manipulating the angry person. Instead—whether you are the distraught parent of a six-year-old who bites, a nurse with a belligerent patient, or a person with a friend who avoids emotional intimacy by constructing a wall of hostility—responding to anger in a way that achieves your goals requires you to focus on yourself.

Much of this workbook focuses on helping you debunk misinformation about anger and discover and change your personal reactions to anger. This preparation gives you the base to develop practical anger-response skills suited to your communication style. Because the focus is on you, not on specific circumstances, the ideas and techniques you'll learn can be used in multiple situations. The nurse who becomes comfortable defusing patients' hostility can use the same method when responding to an antagonistic grocery clerk or a nagging mother or an overly critical life partner. The manager who obtains positive responses from employees can follow those same guidelines to gain similar results with his children, his friends, and his superiors.

As you work the exercises in this book, you will move beyond the spontaneous, conditioned reaction that currently dominates your response to anger. You will create for yourself the freedom to choose how you respond to angry people. Then you will be ready to decide on the methods of responding to anger that work best for you.

The *Responding to Anger* workbook is about you taking control of your reactions so you can make decisions that put you in control of your behavior throughout your life.

I

Personal Responses to Another's Anger

ANGER IS A COMMON EMOTION. Most people encounter angry feelings of varying intensity every day, many times a day. How, or if, this emotion is expressed may differ from person to person or situation to situation. Some people spontaneously blurt out their angry feelings. Others hide their anger behind a forced smile while planning revenge. Still others may be angry and not know it. Since anger is such a common emotional experience, the ability to recognize it in others and respond to it effectively is a skill that can produce rich dividends in all your relationships, whether personal or professional. Unfortunately, it is seldom taught.

Once when I was facilitating an adolescent group therapy session, a group member, Dave, turned to another member, Dorothy, to say he was angry with her about something she had done. She replied, "Well, that's your problem." Disgusted, Dave snarled back, "Jeez, thanks." Dorothy looked at me and asked, "Well, what am I supposed to say when he tells me he's angry?"

Dorothy's question was not only timely and pertinent, but also indicative of a problem experienced by people of all ages, at all levels of intelligence, and in a variety of life circumstances. Recently I watched a salesman trying to calm an irate customer by reciting the proper procedures for returning merchandise. The more he talked, the angrier she became. A therapist friend once told me that she did not want to see a certain client because all he did during their sessions was "spew angry epithets about his wife" and resist when asked to talk about himself. Sometimes parents react to their children's anger with a scolding, or worse, a slap, not realizing that they haven't removed their child's ire, but merely squelched it. The child's angry feelings remain hidden just below the surface, waiting to emerge later.

Dorothy's question, simple and specific, focused on a dilemma many people experience: What do we do when someone is angry? The answer is not simple, nor does one specific answer apply to everyone in the same situation. Instead, once we understand the dynamics of anger, we have the ability to choose an appropriate response style suited to our personality and the incident.

To respond to another person's anger effectively, we need to take various factors into account. I usually ask four questions:

1. Is there a high probability that the other person's anger will escalate to physical aggression?
2. What would you like the outcome to be?
3. What is the social context?
4. How can your response be worded so it feels natural to your way of speaking?

The first consideration is safety. *Is there a high probability that the other person's anger will escalate to physical aggression?* If so, leave! No one deserves to be another person's punching bag. No one has to remain in a place or near a person when danger is an imminent possibility. Get away from the source of potential danger!

After Dorothy replied that she was not afraid Dave would become violent, I asked, *"What would you like the outcome to be?"* If she wanted Dave to remain angry, grumble, and shut up, then her response to his anger was effective. But if her goal was to provide information, and she needed him to listen and understand, then she would need to try a different response. If Dorothy wanted to initiate a dialogue that would enhance their relationship, then she would need still another response.

The third consideration strongly influences the second: *What is the social context?* The situation, environment, and relationship of the people involved shape the parameters of socially acceptable behaviors, including interactions that contain anger. A mother may react one way to her irate child in a grocery store and another way at home. Friends respond differently to each other's anger when playing touch football than during a business meeting with their colleagues and boss.

The final consideration involves personality. *How can your response be worded so it feels natural to your way of speaking?* It is important that Dorothy, in responding to Dave's anger, feels comfortable with the words and actions she chooses.

In the group that day, Dorothy chose to begin a dialogue that might enhance her relationship with Dave. I explained that she needed to let him know she could tell he was angry and that she could start by explaining how she had interpreted what Dave had told her. She replied, "He is angry because I broke his trust." I asked her to be more specific: "Did you break his trust or does he only think you broke his trust?" She responded, "That's what he's thinking." I suggested that Dorothy put her interpretation of what Dave was angry about into a question, using her own words, and ask him. So she looked at Dave and asked, "Are you angry because you think I broke your trust?" Her question let him know that his anger had been communicated. It was no longer an issue. What remained for discussion was what triggered the anger.

At this point, it did not matter whether Dave answered yes or no. Either response would have become a springboard for a dialogue that would enhance the relationship. Dave's response was yes, which gave Dorothy the opportunity to talk about what she had done and why, explaining that she did not realize her actions would violate his trust. If Dave had responded no to her question, Dorothy could have asked him, again using her own words, for more information about how he had interpreted her behavior.

Will Dorothy use this process in a spontaneous incident outside group therapy? She is, after all, an intelligent, high-functioning adolescent who is capable of reviewing and understanding the step-by-step procedures used to respond to Dave's anger. Unfortunately, the answer is probably not—at least, not yet.

Group therapy is a safe setting, where coaches can help Dorothy slow down, think, and then act. Her tendency to reply in a manner that shuts off further communication is an immediate, conditioned response. In an everyday situation, where she may not feel as safe and where there are no coaches, her years of conditioning will likely override the new process she has learned. Without more work, when her mother yells or her sister has a temper tantrum or her boyfriend pouts, Dorothy will find herself repeating the more familiar behavior.

Learning to respond to anger in a new way that will become spontaneous and natural during a stressful encounter can be done. It takes time, self-honesty, and the willingness to practice, stumble, and practice some more. With effort, success will come.

When I first started trying out new ways to respond to anger, I felt awkward and uncomfortable. Sometimes, halfway through an angry interchange, I would automatically revert to my old way, and aggressive words flew from my mouth. No one really won when I did this. One of us would feel bullied and the other would be remorseful for having bullied. I would feel disheartened and wonder, "Will I ever get this right?" At those times I was tempted to throw my hands up and say, "To heck with it. It's just not worth it." When I had a little more time to think, my original motivation for change would creep its way back into my conscious thoughts.

My response to angry people had always been sarcasm and combativeness. It created a chasm between us. It pushed them away. What I really yearned for was closeness and emotional intimacy, a lessening of the distance between us. With that in mind, I would return to the work of practicing a new way. I would review the angry incident and determine what I could have done differently. I would then rehearse the new behavior mentally until I was sure it would be at my disposal next time.

Finally my efforts paid off. I was able to respond consistently in the ways I wanted. I was in control of my own behavior. I reacted in ways that helped others lower their anger, and I encouraged them to communicate what was behind that anger. My relationships with those around me became deeper and closer.

Your reaction to other people's anger may be different than mine. Instead of an aggressive response style, perhaps you tend to have a depressive style, finding ways to avoid or tune out other people when they are angry. The result is the same. You create a distance between yourself and others. Again, no one wins. The angry person knows she has not been heard or understood. Even worse, she may think you do not care enough to respond. You, aware of the other person's anger, are left with personal uncertainties and the continuing need to avoid that person.

DISCOVERING YOUR CURRENT RESPONSE STYLE

Whether your response style is to fight or to avoid someone else's anger, the process for changing that style is the same. It begins with investigating your expectations of what you can do when someone is angry. The next task in the process of change is to explore how you learned to emotionally or physically survive the ravages of misused anger.

The following exercises will help you with this process. As you complete them, be honest. The one "right" answer is *your* answer. You will use that response later in the book to understand how your emotional and behavioral reactions to other people's angry feelings are based on misconceptions about anger that impede your ability to respond productively.

Don't limit yourself to the space provided on these pages. A notebook may be helpful for doing the exercises more completely and for writing down ideas as you read this book.

What Were Your Initial Lessons?

Children learn about anger by watching angry adults, especially their caregivers. Children internalize their impressions about what they see, and these ideas become the foundation for their own future reactions. They tend to mimic the adults in their lives—that's how they learn to act in given situations.

Remember a time during your childhood when your primary caregivers were angry with each other. How did you know that at least one was angry? What was said or done?

How did the person receiving the anger react?

What happened next?

As you watched or listened to the anger, what were some of your thoughts and how did you feel?

What did you do?

What was the outcome of the angry incident?

What Are Your Emotional Reactions?

The strongest learning experiences involving a person's psyche and emotions occur during traumatic events. Determining whether an event is traumatic depends upon the participant's perspective of the incident. From a child's point of view, a caregiver's rageful anger, if expressed with threats, violence, or the removal of love, can be a traumatic event that creates powerful mental and emotional reactions. If a number of similar events occur, the consequent reactions become expectations with the potential to recur every time someone within your presence is angry.

Relate a time when you were a child and your mother (or other female caregiver) became very angry with you.

What event triggered her anger?

What did she say or do while angry?

What were your feelings and thoughts as she expressed her anger?

What did you do or say?

Relate a time when you were a child that your father (or other male caregiver) became very angry with you.

What event triggered his anger?

What did he say or do?

What were your feelings and thoughts as he expressed his anger?

What did you do or say?

What Incidents Created Your Response Style?

A person's basic response to anger develops during childhood. This style modifies and expands as a child grows, meets new people, and participates in novel life experiences.

List incidents when others became angry with you, from when you were a toddler until you became an adult. Include your primary caregivers, teachers, friends, siblings, and even strangers if the event was significant. Choose three angry events, one from each of three different stages of your life, such as childhood, adolescence, and adulthood. If you have a difficult time remembering, ask others who may be familiar with some events in your life. Then indicate what the angry person said or did and how you responded.

Event 1: Who was angry and what triggered that anger?

What did that person say or do?

What did you do?

Event 2: Who was angry and what triggered that anger?

What did that person say or do?

What did you do?

Event 3: Who was angry and what triggered that anger?

What did that person say or do?

What did you do?

How Do You Respond to Anger?

A child learns to experience an internal, emotional reaction to other people's anger. This reaction produces a behavioral response. As the child grows older, the emotions triggered by another's anger remain the same, but the behavioral response changes and develops into an adult version of the early style. By adulthood, individuals have made a variety of modifications that enable different responses for different people in different social settings.

As you provide examples below of how you respond to anger now, it is important that you include incidents that involve different people—your spouse or partner, your children, your boss, a co-worker, a friend, clients.

When   is angry with me:

My internal reactions (thoughts and feelings) are

My external response (action) is

When   is angry with me:

My internal reactions (thoughts and feelings) are

My external response (action) is

When   is angry with me:

My internal reactions (thoughts and feelings) are

My external response (action) is

When   is angry with me:

My internal reactions (thoughts and feelings) are

My external response (action) is

What Is Your Mental Reenactment?

Normally after an angry exchange that remains unresolved, we mentally re-live the incident. During these subsequent reenactments, ideas of what could have been done, should have been done, or might be done next time wend their way into the replayed incident and produce a new scenario. Using incidents that involve different people:

Describe a time when someone expressed anger toward you.

How did you reenact this event?

Describe a time when someone expressed anger toward you.

How did you reenact this event?

Describe a time when someone expressed anger toward you.

How did you reenact this event?

What Is Your Ideal Response?

What do you think is an ideal, healthy response to another's anger? As with previous questions, you may need to think about how this question applies to various relationships in your life. For instance, you may determine that the ideal response with your children would be different than the ideal response with your customers.

My ideal response to _____'s anger would be

My ideal response to _____'s anger would be

My ideal response to _____'s anger would be

My ideal response to _____'s anger would be

My ideal response to _____'s anger would be

WHAT YOUR ANSWERS INDICATE

Having completed the preceding exercises, you have put some thought and energy into looking at how you respond to other people's anger and the process you went through to develop your response style. The questions required effort to answer. Perhaps it was difficult to remember specific situations. You may have reviewed some painful incidents that occurred long ago. You even may have asked others for help. But this effort may already be paying you dividends. By answering the questions honestly and thoroughly, you may be starting to understand the pattern of behaviors that you use to respond to anger.

Equally important, you may be developing an awareness of how your responses are triggered by longstanding internal reactions. These internal reactions, the thoughts and feelings originally precipitated by angry adults, were appropriate and useful to you when you were a youngster. In fact, they may have been necessary for your safety. But they were developed from the perspective of a vulnerable child. You are no longer that vulnerable and dependent child, and the thoughts and feelings of your youth may be counterproductive to you as an adult. The greater awareness you have of these internal reactions and how they developed, the more skilled you will be at recognizing them when they occur and replacing them with more helpful reactions.

What Were Your Initial Lessons?

Before you could talk you began acquiring the knowledge you now have about anger and how to respond when someone is angry. You did this by observing your parents interact. If they expressed their angry feelings in loud arguments with hateful words and hurt feelings, you may not have understood the exact meaning of what was said or what was going on, but you were able to experience the intensity of the situation. And you were able to assimilate that intensity as an unpleasant occurrence to be avoided. If violent actions accompanied the loud, hurtful words, then the emotional tension and unpleasantness was that much greater.

Even if the arguing or anger incidents in your home were devoid of raised voices, the angry feelings of your parents may have left a negative impression on you. Anger is a powerful emotion, typified by physical, muscular tension. This tension can be so strong that people can sense another's anger even when it is not externalized by a covert behavior. Because infants, toddlers, and school-aged children are vulnerable to the world around them and dependent on their caregivers for survival, they are especially tuned in to their parents' feelings, tensions, and mood swings.

If, for instance, a mother uses her anger to punish a child's father by ignoring him for prolonged periods, and the father responds by ignoring her in return, leaving the house, or "getting even" somehow, the children experience the tension in the household. They probably feel a number of uncomfortable feelings generated from not knowing what would result from the silent punishments their parents administered to each other.

In some homes, anger is rarely expressed openly. Parents go behind closed doors when they have heated disagreements or leave the room when they feel angry. If your home was like this when you were growing up, you may have missed the opportunity to observe how to resolve conflict, how to express anger assertively, and how to respond to anger in ways that encourage deeper communication.

At around age three, most children begin imitating what they see and hear from the people around them. I will never forget the mortified look on my friend's face as she watched her five-year-old daughter playing house with a friend. The girl stood with one hand on her hip and the other extended with the index finger pointed at her friend: "You should know better than to do that without telling me first. How am I supposed to . . ." The girl's gestures were my friend's from the previous evening. The words came from an argument my friend had had with her husband about the balance in their checking account. My friend's daughter was engaging in the process used by children to learn social interaction skills.

You went through the same process when learning how to respond to anger. You saw or heard how your parents or others responded to someone's anger. During play you mimicked what you had seen, and then you incorporated the response into your reservoir of potential behaviors. From then on, the response style you practiced during play became available for use.

What Were Your Emotional Reactions?

Some people have trouble answering the questions in this chapter. If this is the case for you, remember two incidents, one for each parent, when you were punished. Anger is often the emotional impetus when parents punish. Also, this is one of the main reasons one individual's anger has the potential to induce strong reactions in another. Punishment meted out by a parent has two components that leave lasting impressions on the child. One is emotional and the other is cognitive.

The first emotional reaction—fear—occurs before punishment begins. Fear warns of potential danger and unpleasantness. If your parents commonly used punishment as discipline, you were conditioned to connect danger or unpleasantness to another person's anger. Your body, wanting to protect you, automatically responded to signs of anger in the environment by generating fear, its internal warning signal. How often and how harsh the punishment was dictates the intensity of the initial fear reaction you experience today. The harshness of the punishment determines the level of unpleasantness or hurt that you expect when someone else is angry.

The cognitive component of punishment is influenced by the situation that triggered the discipline, the type of punishment, the words spoken by the punishing parent, and how you interpreted and internalized them. If your parents yelled and called you names when you made a mistake, then you learned that people get angry and hurt you for your mistakes.

I witnessed an extreme example when I worked at a treatment center for addicted women with children. One of the residents, Clarisse, heard a crash come from her bedroom. She ran in and saw her favorite bottle of perfume shattered on the floor. Her son stood over the aromatic mess, created when he knocked into the bureau, causing the bottle to fall. By the time I arrived, Clarisse had her left hand clamped around her son's upper arm to hold him in place so she could use her right hand to flail away at him with a leather shoe. All the while, she was yelling at the four-year-old boy. I walked in on "You stupid little shit."

Clarisse was in the process of teaching her son two lessons about anger: People will get angry when he has an accident, and when people are angry, they will hurt him. Clarisse's words, uttered during a traumatic moment for her son, taught him a third, perhaps more destructive, lesson that will also influence his responses to other people's anger. Her words were teaching him to evaluate himself as stupid. If he internalized this judgment into his self-concept, he will tend to interpret what other people say when angry as calling him stupid. He will do this even when people have no intention of judging him as such and have not given the slightest indication that they think he is stupid. If he has been taught that he is stupid, he believes he is stupid, and he expects others, when angry, to call him stupid. He will hear them label him as stupid, even when they don't.

Not all parents, when angry, yell or hit their children. Perhaps your parents sent you off to your room. Maybe your mother gave you the silent treatment and ignored you for awhile. Even these forms of punishment can present problems, depending on how you interpreted your mother's behavior and then internalized it into your self-concept. What message did you get about your worth as a family member when you were confined to your room while the rest of the family was together? What ideas did you get about your personal worth when the one you depended on the most for love and nurturing acted as though you didn't exist? Some people learn to think: I'm not important, I don't exist, I'm not good enough, I'm bad, or I'm worthless.

Once you become aware of how you interpreted your parents' angry, punishing behavior as a reflection of your self-concept, you can learn to respond more effectively to anger. Without this awareness, you will respond to another's anger through the distortion created by an internalized interpretation.

How Did Your Response Style Develop?

From birth until the moment their brains stop functioning, people continually observe their world and process new observations according to information they gathered in their previous experiences. Infants perform this process using their senses and no understanding. A baby's social world is very small, usually including their primary caregivers and a few family members. Once they are old enough to move about and to understand language, they take an active role in learning social behaviors by imitating those around them. Four-year-olds mimic how others express anger and how others respond to anger. When children reach school age and head off to kindergarten, their response style is already in place.

How Do You Respond to Anger?

A number of research studies done in the late 1970s and early 1980s show that 60 percent of three-year-olds who were rated as aggressive maintained that rating at eight years of age. Sixty percent of those eight-year-olds were rated again as aggressive when retested between the ages of twelve and fourteen. But when tested again when they were between sixteen and eighteen years old, only 20 percent were rated as aggressive.[1]

A 40 percent drop seems significant enough to say that aggressive individuals, at least in the teen years, can learn new ways to express and respond to anger. This may have happened for you. Perhaps during your adolescence, you came to realize that aggressive responses, even when provoked, were unacceptable to your new peer group. Or perhaps you looked around and realized that people who did not respond to anger with aggression left conflicts with fewer emotional or physical scars. And so, as you entered adulthood, you tried new, less hurtful behaviors.

From childhood on, your world has been expanding. Some of you may have gone to college or married and moved away from your childhood surroundings. In doing so, you may have met new people and encountered new ideas that bolstered your self-esteem and encouraged you to stand up for yourself and what you believe in. You may have watched your new friends assert themselves without aggression or withdrawal in the face of another's anger and obtain their goals. It seemed to work well for them, so you incorporated some of their behaviors into your repertoire of potential responses.

For most of you, the least that happened was that you modified your behavioral response from that typically used by a child to one that is acceptable for an adult. But your internal reaction, the emotional stimulation that occurs when you are confronted with another's angry outburst, has not changed, nor has your basic response style. The internal reaction still happens and the resultant behavior is still there—it is just dressed up in adult clothing.

If you ran and hid when faced with parental anger, you probably withdraw and hide now. It is not socially acceptable for an adult to go running from the room when someone is angry or to sit in a corner and cry. So, instead, you escape or pout by using more subtle means such as ignoring the outburst, changing the subject, avoiding eye contact, or limiting future contact with the person.

Another response is to become very placating. It is almost as though you want peace at any expense. You apologize often for things you cannot control or did not do. Someone gets angry, and your first words are, "I'm sorry."

If you were aggressive as a child, you may still be aggressive, or you may have modified the overtly aggressive behaviors into the more hidden or acceptable styles of punishment or argument. Punishment has a strong flavor of revenge. When someone is angry with you, you react by feeling anger. You hold on to that anger until you can get away and figure out how to get even.

A young man I know worked at an ice cream parlor. One day his boss became angry because he did not display the tubs of ice cream the way she wanted. She expressed her anger in a loud, long tirade. The young man, although furious, said nothing but, "Yes, ma'am, I'll fix it." Later, the young man, still seething from the boss's harsh words, looked around to make sure he was alone, opened his pants, and peed in the tub of vanilla ice cream.

If you take the combative approach in answer to another's anger, you tend to argue. You find yourself in verbal duels throughout your day. You may notice that you constantly search for flaws in other people's ideas and actions. You often describe others as idiots or stupid. Perhaps you tell people off, using sarcasm and a rapier wit. Your life may seem like one continuous battle.

Triangulation—engaging a third person with more power to intervene— is not as acceptable for adults as it is for children. To maintain a safe and violence-free environment, teachers and parents may encourage children to seek out an adult when they witness angry outbursts. Children tend to stop using triangulation during adolescence, however. Teenagers, as they struggle with the developmental task of separation from parents, view adults as adversaries. Teens who report a peer's aggressive outburst to an adult in authority risk being tagged as a snitch, squealer, narc, or rat. Not all teenagers adhere to this norm of "don't tell." Nor do all the individuals who follow the "don't tell" norm during their adolescent years bring it with them into adulthood. As a supervisor, I have had many competent workers complain to me about angry co-workers who verbally let them have it. I once counseled a woman whose daughter-in-law would often call to say, "Do you know what your son said to me today?" and would then go on a tear about how he had gotten angry about something she had done or failed to do.

These responses to another person's anger are not necessarily wrong or bad. The question to ask yourself is, "Do they accomplish my goal?" If your goal is to defuse a potentially aggressive episode, responses such as placating, combativeness, triangulation, or withdrawal may work. If your goal is to develop greater understanding with the other person or greater intimacy, all of these responses will defeat your efforts. They all tend to put either distance or another person between you and the one who is angry.

There is a response style that involves negotiation, and it has merit when it is used to defuse an angry situation. Many adult couples, co-workers, or groups of people use this response effectively as a means to obtain mutually satisfying solutions. But the act of defusing anger does not always involve communication that enhances intimacy. Therefore, if you are looking to strengthen a personal relationship, this response also has its limitations.

You may have noticed that your responses differ depending upon whose anger you were facing. A general rule of thumb is that overt aggression flows downward from the more powerful to those with lesser power. In other words, you are more likely to make a combative response to your child's anger than you are to your supervisor's anger.

What Is Your Mental Reenactment?

After leaving an angry encounter, it is difficult to put it out of your thoughts. People tend to relive the incident mentally, sometimes embellishing the event to make themselves look better or to make the other person look worse. Sometimes the mental replay can even become a totally rewritten script, outlining what you could have said or what you will do next time. Examining the scripts you replay can be very helpful in two ways. They can guide you to an understanding of the power you give to other people's anger, and, in some instances, they can assist you in determining the goals you want to achieve from similar encounters.

Most people give far more power to other people's anger than it deserves. If, for example, your co-worker expressed his anger about something you had done, and you left the incident trembling with fear, then your expectations of what his anger might do to you were greater than the reality of what his anger actually did. When you got back to your office and replayed the incident, did your fear turn to anger? Did you envision yourself telling him off, getting even, or giving him a good smack in the mouth? If so, then you give anger the power to punish, to hurt, to be used as a weapon for revenge. This is what you expect from anger, whether it is yours or someone else's.

Perhaps you did not leave your co-worker's office trembling with fear. You may have responded to his anger by becoming angry and verbally aggressive. You told him off. When you returned to your office, you reviewed the episode, highlighting all the things he said that were inaccurate, all the ways that he was wrong. In this scenario, you have given anger the power to judge. The judgment, in this situation, is not just about your having performed a task below someone else's standards. The high level of defensiveness indicates that you have interpreted the anger as a judgment. To you, your co-worker's anger is not saying that you have done something wrong; it is saying that you are somehow defective as a human being. You have given the other person's anger the power to attack your sense of self-worth.

Or are you a person who might have responded to this co-worker's anger with an abusive outburst and, upon returning to your desk and reviewing what was said, proceeded to denigrate yourself for the harsh words that flew out of your mouth? Maybe you promised yourself that next time would be different, next time you would bite your tongue. You would think first. You would act rationally.

You could be similar to one of my clients who envisioned different scenarios for different people. She said that after an angry episode with her husband, she would imagine all the ways she could make his life miserable. After blowing up at her four-year-old daughter, she would mentally berate herself and then construct ways that she would make it up to the child the next day.

A close examination of your scenarios can help you develop some possible goals that would lead to more satisfying results. If you related with the first example, your goal, when encountering another person's anger, might be to reduce your fear to a level that would allow you to stand up for yourself. In the second example, your goal might be to express your own anger in such a way that you could walk away from the situation feeling okay about the way you handled it. Or perhaps, like the mother in the third example, who hurled harsh words at her angry daughter and then felt guilty about it, you want to respond to your child's anger in a way that would be beneficial to the youngster.

What Is Your Ideal Response?

Often the ideal response to anger depends upon the circumstance and people involved. People concerned with responding to anger in a business situation often want to remain calm and stay in control. Spouses want to be able to let their partner vent their anger, and people in the helping professions often name that as their ideal response as well. Parents seem to favor a response that explains the anger away.

There is nothing inherently wrong with any of these ideal responses. The problem is, they can be counterproductive to what you are trying to achieve. In a business situation, it can be helpful to remain calm and in control of yourself. If you want to extend your control to the entire interchange, however, and the other business party is aware of it, you may discover that he becomes more irate. His anger may be generated by the fear that he has no control or power and that he suspects you will take advantage of him. His anger is an attempt to gain power and protect his interests. The more you demonstrate control, the more he resists by increasing his anger.

In situations that involve intimate partners, if the goal is to create greater intimacy, encouraging each other to vent anger can defeat the purpose. One important, if not the major, function of anger is to defend and protect. Anger builds an emotional wall that hides more vulnerable feelings. Studies as far back as the 1970s,[2] as well as more recent studies,[3] indicate that when angry feelings are allowed to spew forth, the anger sensation increases rather than decreases. Venting anger merely strengthens the wall of anger that blocks the way to deeper intimacy.

Responding to their children's angry outbursts has to be one of the most difficult situations that parents encounter on a regular basis. Different incidents of anger from children require different responses. If a young person's anger has been triggered because she misunderstood a certain event, then an explanation may help. When the child is able to attribute a new meaning to the event, a feeling other than anger may emerge. But different situations may require different responses. Say you sent your daughter to her room because she took her baby brother's candy. Now she is angry about being punished. Anger is a normal feeling to have when punished. Who among us does not feel angry when a punishment is levied upon us, even when we know the reason?

More than two and a half years ago, I was driving from South Carolina to Virginia to visit a friend in the last stage of liver cancer. I very much wanted to see him before he died. I chose to speed. I knew the consequences and decided the risk was worth it. I got caught. When I appeared before the magistrate, she gave me a long explanation about how the state was cracking down on speeding to reduce vehicular deaths. I understood that I had broken the law and I understood her explanation. I still felt angry when I paid the eighty-eight-dollar fine. I felt even angrier when I received my next insurance premium and it was twice as high as what I had been paying. Now, almost three years later, I still feel a twinge of ire when I write out a check for the higher premium.

My point is that there are times when anger is the expected, natural emotion to a given situation. If a parent wants her child to be able to experience, express, and use her anger productively in those situations, constantly trying to explain it away will not achieve that result. Instead the child learns that anger is to be rationalized away.

What is the most productive way for a mother to respond to her angry child? How can one worker forge an alliance with an irate co-worker? What can a spouse do to turn his partner's anger toward a more intimate interchange? A number of practical techniques are designed to accomplish these goals, but they are difficult to implement when they are competing with years of an already deeply engrained response pattern. Therefore, if you want to respond to other people's anger effectively, you must first reduce the impact of your existing style.

Remember, your current response style is based on a lifelong process that began in very early childhood with your internal, emotional reactions and the cognitive misinformation you gained from observing and participating in social interactions. Your response style was then reinforced by years of repeated use and refined by a number of adaptive modifications.

Lessening your tendency to use this more familiar response during the heightened emotionality involved in an angry encounter is no easy feat. It can be done, but to do so requires a process of personal investigation and work. The first step is to become more comfortable with anger in general. This begins by uncovering the misinformation you have learned throughout the years and replacing it with a more accurate understanding of what anger is all about.

2

The Many Uses and
Misuses of Anger

ANGER IS A BASIC HUMAN EMOTIONAL RESPONSE; it is neither good nor bad. To place judgments on anger, or, for that matter, on any emotional reaction, is counterproductive. Emotionally healthy human beings experience feelings continuously throughout the day. Even though each emotion has a unique function, all emotions have one purpose in common: to provide information about every incident encountered. In this capacity, each of the seven basic emotions—happiness, guilt, sadness, loneliness, inadequacy, fear, and anger—functions as an indicator. Happiness indicates that this is fun, let's keep doing it. Guilt indicates that our behavior has gone contrary to our beliefs or values. Sadness alerts us to appreciate people and things before they are gone. Loneliness cues us to the need for human contact. Inadequacy highlights areas where personal improvements are needed. Fear sounds the danger alarm. Anger says it is time to protect.

The act of judging a feeling diminishes the emotion's functional capabilities. Many people assess emotions by separating them into two categories: those considered good, or worthy of pursuit, and those that are bad, or meant to be avoided. The first category contains happiness and similar emotions, while the second consists of all other feelings, including anger. Some of us put most of our energy into seeking the first category and avoiding the second. Sometimes we are not aware of or choose to ignore feelings that provide information about our environmental circumstances. A valuable source of internal information is unavailable to help us interpret circumstances and make decisions.

Feelings are natural and the ability to use them is instinctive. The desire to seek some and ignore others is taught through a socialization process. Families, churches, media, and schools contribute to this cultural training process. The lessons may be presented in a subtle manner, such as a disapproving scowl from a parent. Or they may be more obvious, such as a group of schoolboys teasing another because he is afraid. Whether subtle or obvious, these social lessons override our instincts and encourage us to avoid or misuse many of our own feelings and to respond negatively to other people's emotional expressions.

Often the lessons we learn are not accurate. An eight-year-old boy who is afraid to jump off the roof of a ten-foot-high building is not a sissy or a coward, as taunted by his friends. He is demonstrating good sense, and he needs to listen to that fear. But he is being taught otherwise and, if he heeds the lesson, he will learn to disparage the fear instead of use it. The same is true for all the emotions placed in the "negative" feeling category, including, if not especially, anger.

One of the more common and harmful lessons taught about anger involves what I call the misappropriation of responsibility. The lesson can be summed up in one sentence: You are responsible for my anger, and I am responsible for yours. This idea is taught and reinforced every time someone says, "You made me angry." The message is clearly that my anger, or lack of anger, depends upon your behavior. So it is up to you to do something that will remove my anger. Someone who buys into this message cannot respond effectively because the angry person is asking for the impossible.

The idea that one person can change another person's feeling is based on erroneous information. No one can reach into another person to flip the on-off switch of an emotional reaction. To respond to another person's anger productively, the responsibility for that anger must be shifted to its proper place, to the person who is experiencing the feeling. The first task in accomplishing this is to understand how anger is defined as an emotion and how it works.

ANGER IS AN INTERNAL REACTION

The phone rings, you pick up the receiver, place it to your ear, and say hello into the mouthpiece. An unknown voice comes through the line, explaining that she is a nurse from the local hospital. Someone you love has been in a serious accident. Your breathing stops and then becomes rapid and shallow. Your palms are sweaty. Your muscles tense. You struggle to stay in control, to stay focused.

If this had really happened, you would be undergoing an *internal reaction*, a biophysiological response. You would be experiencing a strong feeling or emotion. The internal reaction and the physical sensations occur because your body increased certain chemicals. The most predominant chemical in this situation is adrenaline. Humans recognize the consequential physical sensations as fear.

The "re-" in *reaction* indicates that the chemicals and the resultant physical sensations are a response *to* something. In the phone call situation, the response is to the information given by the voice on the phone.

The phone call, with the information it contained, is an *external event*. This is usually the case. But feelings may occur without an external stimulus when a biophysiological, chemical imbalance is present within the human body. This imbalance can be caused by something as minor as hunger, which produces a nervous feeling, or as major as the imbalance responsible for manic-depression, a serious illness with vast mood swings. Whether the internal reaction is triggered by an external event or a biologically based chemical imbalance, correct the chemical imbalance and the emotion fades. When we daydream, fantasize, or imagine, we create emotions by using our minds. We think of an incident or create a scenario in our minds and then experience emotional responses to these mental images.

Defining an emotion as an internal reaction to an external event is adequate only when discussing animals other than humans. At this bestial level, feelings are instinctive and used most often for physical survival. Human beings still function using this primitive ability. It comes from what can be called the "old brain" and is experienced most intensely during times of immediate danger, when survival depends on action without thought.

Through evolution, the human mind has developed what can be considered an additional brain. This "new brain," the neocortex, provides us with the ability to abstract, symbolize, and convey information. With this development, we gained the ability to think about, differentiate, label, and verbally communicate various internal reactions. It is what sets us apart from other animals. My dog cannot come home after a hard day of dog work, sit in her favorite spot, and ruminate about the internal reaction she had when the huge monster dog down the street chased her for three blocks. My dog felt that sensation and then ran. It was all about instinct and survival. But because the neocortex is not about instinct, this higher function must be learned. With this learning, emotions take on a dimension that requires socialization.

We learn to give a name to our internal reactions. This labeling involves experiencing, differentiating, and naming each biophysiological sensation. This is a complex process, and learning it starts at a young age. Children, by the age of six, are developmentally capable of labeling and expressing the four most basic feelings with the descriptive words of *mad, glad, sad,* and *afraid.*[1] Because youngsters have to learn the names for each feeling sensation, they need teachers—the people immediately involved in their lives.

We can use this understanding of emotion to develop a definition of anger:

> Anger is an internal reaction
> (that a person learns to name)
> to an external event.

The emotional process of anger is straightforward and physically based: Something happens. The brain interprets the event in such a way, accurately or not, that it directs the body to produce the chemical that increases the heart and pulse rate, quickens breathing, makes the skin flush, increases muscle tension and body temperature, and activates sweat glands. Metabolism speeds up and the body responds accordingly. The person labels the complete experience "anger."

The important point is that anger, like any other emotion, is the body's internal response to the release of a natural chemical, a hormone. Thoroughly understanding this point will help you respond to other people's anger more effectively for two reasons. First, realizing that anger in itself is not dangerous, threatening, or hurtful removes much of the emotion's potency. Second, understanding what anger is clearly indicates where the responsibility for anger lies. If someone is angry with you, the anger is her chemical, physical response. It is her internal reaction. You cannot reach inside and change the reaction. Although you may choose actions that influence the external event, ultimately only the person experiencing the anger can change the internal response.

MISINFORMATION ABOUT ANGER

In order to choose your response to another person's anger, it is important that you not be trapped into responding out of misinformation you've gathered during your lifetime. Some misinformation strongly influences your emotions because it was presented in powerful, sometimes traumatic, ways. In those cases, the simple act of gaining new information about anger is not potent enough to change your emotional reaction to another person's rage. But you can begin by intellectually replacing the misinformation that you have been given. This will enable you to look at anger in a more positive way. In chapter 5, you can do some exercises designed to assist you in changing your more resistant emotional reactions.

Most cultures engender many misconceptions about anger. Of all our emotions, anger is the one that has the most taboos restraining its expression and the most erroneous information concerning what it is and how to use it. This situation creates discomfort for a person encountering another's angry feelings.

To respond effectively to anger, you need to increase your comfort level around angry feelings. You can increase your awareness of inaccurate ideas about anger and replace them with factual concepts about this powerful emotional response.

The following statements counter the most common misleading ideas about anger propagated by our society.

Anger is not an accusation. You may have discovered in chapter 1 that an accusation of wrongdoing accompanied your caretaker's anger toward you. If this happened often enough, you learned through your experiences that anger is an accusation, and consequently your first reaction to anger is to respond as though you are being blamed for a misdeed.

Although anger is not an accusation, it may be accompanied by an accusation. The accusation is the angry person's interpretation of the external event. In this scenario, the external event would be your behavior. Anger can occur and be expressed without any accusations when all parties take responsibility for their own internal reactions.

Anger is not a sin, and a person who feels angry is not bad because of it. I have heard anger called un-Christian. Some people believe that experiencing anger means they are not living a Christian life. Think about the emotional state of Jesus when he went into the temple and overturned tables. He was not happy nor accepting when he did that. He was quite angry. Not one of the people I have pointed this out to is willing to say that Jesus was in a state of sin or that he was a bad person because he felt angry.

Anger is not a behavior. Often people confuse anger with aggression. Aggression is a behavior. It is one way that people may choose to express anger. They could choose instead from a number of other behaviors besides aggression. Likewise, anger is not violence. Violence is a descriptive category of behaviors. Anger is the internal reaction, and behaviors are the external expression of that reaction. If you understand that, then you know that it is not the other person's anger that gives you problems. Your difficulty in responding to them has to do with the behaviors they may use to express their angry feelings. As an adult, you encounter many people who feel angry. Few of them express that anger with aggression or violence.

Anger is not a weapon. Many parents, without realizing it, methodically set their children up to fear anger in the same way they might fear a weapon. The process consists of these steps: (1) The child does something that the parent does not like. (2) The parent feels angry and expresses it by physically hurting or verbally berating the child. (3) This behavior is repeated, and the child quickly learns to make an anger-pain connection. (4) From then on, the parent wields anger as a weapon of intimidation by announcing, in a threatening tone, "I'm getting angry." The expected outcome is similar to brandishing a gun: Do this or I will shoot. Do this or I will get angry. Anger has become the vehicle of hurt.

Another similar inaccurate impression of anger is the expectation that angry feelings result in punishment. It reminds me of a time about five years ago when a worker's error cost our company about six thousand dollars in Medicaid reimbursement. I felt angry about the situation. I called the worker in, I expressed my anger, and then we talked about what happened and how he could avoid the mistake in the future. He left my office and all seemed well. Two days later he returned, stood in my doorway, and asked, "Well?" I looked at him quizzically. He added, "When are you going to get me?" I asked, "For what?" He replied, "For that Medicaid thing. What disciplinary action are you taking?" After a half hour of talking, I finally convinced him I had no intention of punishing him. I told him that discipline means to teach and that I thought he had already learned how to avoid the same mistake in the future. "And so," I asked, "Why would I punish you?" He looked at me as though I were an alien who had no understanding about Earth before he replied, "Because you were very angry."

Anger is not an evaluation of your worth as a person. Because another human being is angry about something you have done, that does not mean that you are worthless, stupid, unimportant, unlovable, or lazy. Many of my clients have heard such messages from their caregivers. And even though many of them have not had contact with their caregivers in years, they respond to expressions of anger as though they are still hearing the same negative evaluations flung at them as children.

Anger is an internal reaction. Another person's internal reaction has nothing to do with your rightness or wrongness as a human being. It has to do with the chemicals being produced by his body because of the way he has interpreted events around him.

Anger is not a gigantic mistake. Nature did not err when it gave people a wide array of feelings, including anger. Every basic emotion was built into the human species so that *Homo sapiens* would survive and flourish. I have already spoken about emotions being indicators, but their function and importance to humanity goes even further. Each feeling is designed to produce an outcome that will increase the probability of survival. For example, loneliness has played a large part in helping our species survive. Human beings are not the strongest, the biggest, or the fastest animals. In more primitive times, humans protected themselves and fought against bigger, stronger, and faster animals by forming societies. Loneliness encourages us to come together in communities. It is the emotion that motivates us to seek out and make alliances with other people.

Anger has also helped humans since primitive times as the feeling state that directs us to fight when attacked by those bigger, stronger, and faster animals. The adrenaline produced by anger temporarily makes people stronger and faster, leveling the odds of combat.

Anger is not hot boiling water, and people are not teapots. This statement alludes to the concept that anger is stored up and added to on a regular basis until it expands to such large proportions that it has to be vented or it will overflow. This idea is such an enticingly simple explanation that even some professional counselors believe it, but the concept has three major flaws. First, anger cannot be stored. Considering the definition of

anger—an internal reaction created by an overproduction of adrenaline—
I asked three physicians if it is possible to carry around an overabundance
of adrenaline. All three assured me that a person who stayed high on adrenaline would be extremely agitated, unable to sleep, and close to crazy within
three days.

Second, under the teapot theory, each outburst of anger a person has
would lower the anger level. If someone had many outbursts of extreme
proportions, the anger would be reduced until it was almost gone, and it
would be a long time, perhaps months or years, before it built up enough to
overflow again. Yet in real life this is not what occurs. Most often, people
who experience episodes of rage are people who routinely express anger
through aggressive behaviors. According to the teapot theory, these are the
people who ought to have spent all their anger. Yet they are the ones who
keep on agressing.

The third flaw in this concept is the idea that anger needs to be vented
to be reduced. Studies done in the 1970s[2] and in the 1990s[3] indicate that
venting angry feelings increases rather than diminishes the physiological
arousal of anger. Anger was not given to humans so they could vent.
Venting fulfills no survival purpose whatsoever. As with every emotion,
anger serves to sustain and enhance life. Anger accomplishes this by providing the ability and strength to defend through physical altercation. When
the altercation is finished, the angry feelings recede, to be reproduced when
necessitated by another danger.

Anger is not a chronic illness that needs to be managed. This concept
may contradict the current fad of anger management workshops, seminars,
counseling, classes, and groups. Anger is an internal reaction whose main
function is to defend the human being. It does not need to be managed.
Instead, anger arousal needs to be identified when it occurs and used effectively, within the given social context, to fulfill its protective function.

INFORMATION ABOUT ANGER

Understanding anger accurately not only will make this emotion seem less
threatening, reducing your spontaneous negative reaction to someone else's
anger, but it will also help you decide how to respond most effectively in specific situations. Once you know how anger can be used, you can determine

what function anger serves for the person expressing it. Then you can respond in a manner that addresses that particular function.

Anger is a survival mechanism. Anger prepares the body for battle. Without it, the human race probably would not have made it to this century, or far fewer people would be alive today. Before guns were in general use in the 1500s, people relied on physical strength for survival. Defending themselves and their families against wild animals or hunting or raising animals for food and clothing required great physical strength. Anger is the emotion that provides additional strength needed when fighting to survive.

I was caught in the "storm of the century" that hit North Carolina by surprise in the winter of 1999. I did not have wood for the fireplace, and when the electricity went off, the house became extremely cold. Roads were impassable. The temperature continued to drop. In my mind, wood became a necessity for survival. Out in my front yard, an old, dead tree had fallen from the weight of the snow. I donned my winter gear and proceeded out the door and through thigh-high snow to that tree. Alone, I began cutting that tree with a handsaw and a small ax. I pushed, I tugged, I hit, I sawed. When I realized that I was getting nowhere fast, I became angry. Muttering and swearing I sawed faster and pushed and tugged harder. I did not feel myself tiring. I did not feel the pain of strained muscles. I cut enough wood to get through the coldest part of the night. It wasn't until I went inside and the adrenaline, the main chemical associated with anger, receded that I felt the weariness and pain.

This anecdote illustrates two survival functions of anger. It gives additional strength when struggling against the elements, and it hides the pain that may occur during that struggle. Because many people in our society rarely face the need to fight physically for survival, we might ask, "How does knowing this particular function of anger help when attempting to respond to another person's ire?" If the human mind *thinks* that its survival is threatened, it will direct the body to respond to that perceived threat.

Young children who are abandoned by one or both parents are a good illustration of this. Because children depend on the adults in their lives to fulfill their survival needs, abandonment means their survival is in danger. The trauma of abandonment can be so intense that the child carries the abandonment/fear-for-survival connection into adulthood, where it can play out in relationships. If a man attempts to break off a serious relationship, he might find himself faced with an enraged woman. You would think from her behavior that she expects to die if he leaves—and that may be exactly what is going on. The man, if he wants to defuse the situation, will have to address the survival function of anger that has been triggered in the woman.

As a mechanism of survival, the body produces the chemical for anger in order to free itself when trapped. Like many animals, when backed into a corner, the human animal prepares to come out fighting. In our current culture, rarely are people literally caught in a trap. But there are many instances when people see themselves locked into life situations and perceive that they are emotionally ensnared. These situations occur in the arenas where we spend most of our time, work and home. I have met hundreds of workers who think they are trapped in dead-end jobs, not qualified for a promotion, and unaware of opportunities beyond their current places of employment. They are very angry workers. I have counseled wives who thought they were tied to their spouses by security and financial needs. I know husbands who believe they are caught in their marriage by their duty to provide for their family. The perception of being trapped creates an intense amount of anger in the people living in these situations. Its purpose is to help them escape their perceived traps.

Anger has many cultural and social functions. Within any given culture, anger can have a number of social functions. For instance, anger almost always acts as a *social regulator* because it is considered the appropriate feeling to have when the norms, mores, and laws of the culture are violated. The stronger the violated norm, the more intense the anger response. This is extremely important to keep in mind when attempting to respond to another person's anger, especially in the United States. The number of differing cultures in the United States is probably the largest in the world. The mores and norms of these cultural groups can have minor nuances or extensive and extreme differences. It is easy for someone from one cultural group to violate a belief or value of another group inadvertently. Even though the violation was unintentional, it may trigger an intensely angry reaction.

I once witnessed a co-worker become irritated and say, "God damn it!" I do not find this terminology particularly offensive, and so I did not give it any thought. But another co-worker was nearby and heard it also. She became very angry because she belonged to a church that taught taking the

Lord's name in vain is not only offensive but a grievous sin. The offended co-worker went to the supervisor and demanded that an action be taken. Her values were violated, and her resultant anger spurred her to take defensive action.

Anger also functions as a *social bond.* When a group of people focus their anger collectively on an outside group, individual, or situation, the shared anger provides a connection for the members of the group. They have a common enemy. A "we" vs. "they" situation is created.[4] To be a member of the "we" group, an individual must be angry with the "they" group. This phenomenon occurs on sports teams and in other situations that have an element of competition, including some work environments. It helps to focus energy. And it can be very productive when the anger is directed toward completing tasks that successfully overtake the competitor.

People at all levels of management need to be aware that this type of social bonding can become destructive if the target of the anger is not a competitor but a member of the organization, such as another work unit, management, or another shift of the same unit. When this happens, the anger needs to be addressed and, at the very least, redirected as soon as possible. If the anger's accompanying energy is not funneled toward a constructive target, the results may be reduced worker morale, increased turnover, and lowered productivity. More onerous outcomes may include active sabotage aimed at company procedures or at the company's product.

Another social role that anger plays is to *mark and maintain physical boundaries.* Even though one function of anger brings people together, it also has the capacity to keep people apart. Humans are territorial animals. We set, and often publicly mark, the borders of our territory to deter those who might violate our personal area or property. If anyone is bold enough to cross these boundaries without invitation, anger prepares us emotionally and physically to defend the violated property. The defense continues until the trespasser leaves our territory by moving back over the boundary or until we are convinced it is safe and to our advantage for that person to stay.

Anger provides motivation when properly channeled. I was counseling a client who had been referred to me because he often experienced angry feelings. One of my first questions had to do with how he expressed his anger. He replied, "I have no trouble with anger. When I feel mad, I go into the backyard and chop down a tree." Anger is the body's energizer. It propels us into action. When that happens, the body's natural response is to find a way to discharge the energy. Unless you need to clear your property, chopping down trees in your backyard is probably not the most productive use of that energy. The real function of anger is to provide the impetus to overcome obstacles that block us from attaining our goals. So unless this client felt angry because he could not get his land cleared, he was misspending the energy created during the anger response.

For anyone's anger to be useful, more must occur than merely experiencing the feeling and releasing the accompanying energy. People who use their anger proficiently undergo a four-step process:

1. They feel the anger.
2. They recognize the situation that provoked it.
3. They identify a healthy, productive goal that would alleviate the situation.
4. They maintain this energizing emotion until they can take at least the first steps toward the goal.

In order to initiate this process, people must nullify the misinformation that says, "You are responsible for my anger." As long as they maintain this idea, their anger and its concurrent energy will be directed at changing the other person and not at reaching personal goals. For this reason, it is important that parents examine how they express their anger and how they respond to their children's anger. The phrase "You make me angry" needs to be removed from a parent's speech. It places blame for the emotion onto the child. When a child is angry, a very effective way for a parent to respond, instead of becoming defensive, is to help the child through the four steps involved in the motivation process.

Anger is a method of communication. Anger always carries a message. The angry adolescent is trying to be heard. The worker who raises her voice in agitation has information to pass on that she thinks is important. The fuming customer is communicating. If the sender does not see any indication that her message has been heard, her anger will likely escalate and the signals of anger—behaviors that let others know angry feelings are strong and just below the surface—will intensify.

Two problems occur that make it difficult for the communication to be heard. The first involves the angry person, the sender of the communiqué.

By the time someone gets angry about a situation, the meaning of the intended message has more than likely become garbled. The second problem involves the receiver, the person who is listening to the angry outburst. Because people have a tendency to react defensively to anger, they do not listen carefully for the meaning under the harsh words. So the listener distorts the message even more.

Fortunately, if you are the receiver and your role in the conversation is to respond, you do not have to understand what the sender is trying to communicate in order to defuse the situation and to begin a dialogue. It is enough to convince the angry person that you are attempting to understand what she is trying to convey. You can simply say, "What you have to say is important and I am trying to understand." Depending on the situation, you might add, "I can listen better if you would slow down" or, "It would help me if you'd lower your voice."

Anger furnishes psychological protection. During group therapy, a client looked at me and said, "I feel angry when you interrupt me like that. I get to thinking I'm not important." This young man's anger acted exactly the way it was meant to act. When he thought he was being put down, his anger came up to protect him. This function of anger is common. Although anger began in primitive beings as a means of physical protection, in our culture, where hand-to-hand combat is relatively uncommon, anger arousal is associated far more often with psychological or emotional protection. It is used to save face, to fight against unfairness, to protect personal identity.

Combining the protective aspect of anger with its communication function provides a major clue to the meaning that the angry feeling is carrying. A response that positively addresses the message can dissipate the anger and invite the angry person to talk on a less defensive level.

3
The Complex Nature of Anger

RECENTLY, A CONTRACTOR CAME TO MY HOME to fix part of my driveway that had washed away with melted snow and a day of torrential rain. As soon as my calico cat heard the voice of a stranger, she bent low to the floor and made a beeline for the bedroom. She hid under the bed and did not come out for hours. This is my cat's normal fear response. She does not think about, rationalize, or analyze it. She does not prepare for it. The fear comes, she runs. It is instinctive.

Human beings can operate on the same instinctive level as my cat, especially when their survival is threatened. But usually their brains function on a more sophisticated level. They have the ability to plan future events or reminisce about past exploits. If someone mentions the song "Angel of the Morning," memories of my high school prom come cascading to mind. With the smell of an antiseptic, I remember the cold, glaringly white operating room of a hospital in New Haven, Connecticut. Very quickly I can change that image by thinking about the stone fireplace that warmed the living room of my former home in Charlotte, North Carolina. These memories, created years and hundreds of miles apart, trigger emotional reactions that intensify as I review the scenes generated within each mental picture. If I like, I can share, in detail, any one or all of these memories and the associated feelings with a friend. This ability is unique to the human species because of our "new brain."

The human mind can do even more. As a person goes through the day, he encounters new situations. Each new incident is processed by drawing on old information. Or if past experiences are not appropriate for the situation, new ways to respond can be sought. Humans can sit down, think about the new situation, call a friend, discuss it, and then make a decision. Each choice that is made will be accompanied by an emotion. The accompanying emotion then becomes available for use in making future decisions.

Obviously, the process of human feelings is much more complex than the instinctive or conditioned responses of other animals. This complexity can interfere with productively using or responding to emotions, because it allows people to judge how they and others feel when they react. When the judgment is negative, people are capable of generating intellectual ways to negate the body's internal reactions or to avoid responding to other people's feeling reactions. Among the many human emotional states, this occurs most often with anger. Therefore, understanding the components of the feeling process increases the response options we can access when facing another person's ire.

COMPONENTS OF THE FEELING PROCESS

In the early 1990s, I wrote in *The Anger Workbook* that some researchers contend that the aggressive expression of anger is biologically based[1] while others argue that aggressive behaviors are socially learned by imitating role models.[2] Views based on equally divergent theories continue to be researched. One study found low levels of the stress hormone cortisol in aggressive boys.[3] These boys were described by other children as the "meanest" in their class. Their aggressive behaviors included starting fights, using weapons, and forcing sexual acts on others. But another highly respected researcher, Kenneth Dodge, has done a number of studies that indicate children use a cognitive process, consisting of five specific steps, to feel and express their anger. He concludes that aggressive behavior is the result of a child's inability to identify and process social cues accurately.[4]

Who is right? Is aggression biological in nature? Is it learned by watching others and then mimicking their behaviors? Or is Dodge correct? Is it about environmental perceptions and cognitive processing? How can anger appear to be so different from one researcher's studies to another's? The answer is simple. They are all correct. As for any emotion, anger and its expression develop through a process. This process consists of five basic components. Each of the researchers investigated a different component. Their conclusions do not negate but rather support each other's findings when viewed in this context.

Anger is one of the most, if not *the* most, complex feelings human beings experience. Understanding anger is facilitated by first creating a foundation of knowledge about emotions in general and their resultant expressions. By adding facts about anger to this foundation, we can comprehend how angry feelings are generated and expressed.

In chapter 2, I defined an emotion as an internal reaction (that a person learns to name) to an external event. This definition states what a feeling is. It does not give an explanation of how it is provoked, how it is expressed, or how it fits into a person's everyday experiences. The feeling itself is neither the beginning event nor end result. It is one element, the emotional component, of a complex process. This process also includes mental and behavioral components. Figure A depicts how the components work together.

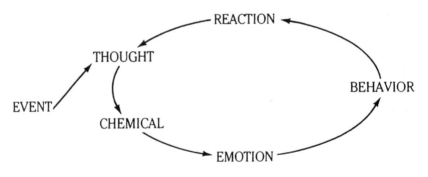

Figure A

This diagram illustrates the circular nature of the feeling process. It portrays the emotion's trigger, the feeling state, and its expression. What the drawing does not show is the enormous input and learning from many sources that must occur for each element to complete its part of the represented circular process.

Event

An emotion begins with an event. Something happens within a person's sensory range that signals the brain. The signaling event could be a long-forgotten song playing on the radio, a traffic jam on the way to an important meeting, or the grumbled "Good morning" of a co-worker. It might be a date that triggers the memory of a friend's death, or perhaps something that occurred earlier in the day has resurfaced and demands attention. Any environmental or mental happening that occurs during waking hours initiates the feeling process.

Anger arousal, when triggered, acts like other emotions. According to researcher Kenneth Dodge, who has studied young children and anger, a person's environment provides cues (similar to events) that indicate the need for an angry reaction to provide protection against a hostile environment.[5]

Thought

Once the brain is alerted to the event, the mind interprets what the event means for that specific person. This component accounts for why different people in the same situation can react with very different feelings. An individual's interpretation is determined by past experiences, the emotions occurring during those past situations, and a personal understanding of the current social setting. These three influential variables can be unique to each person, resulting in three different meanings for the event. A person who has a wide array of life experiences, understands the emotional reactions those experiences engendered, and possesses a strong knowledge of the involved social norms has the highest probability of making an accurate interpretation.

Dodge points out that an anger reaction is appropriate if a child has registered threatening environmental cues accurately and realized that she needs to defend herself.[6] I believe Dodge's theory goes beyond children. I think it applies to adults as well.

If the event is a memory, the event has already been translated. The mental recall of the situation may develop new insight, leading to a reinterpretation of the event. Whether the event originates from an external situation or an internal memory or whether the interpretation is accurate or inaccurate, an immense amount of mental activity has taken place in a very short time. And from this activity, a predominant thought emerges.

Chemical

The predominant thought that arises from the event triggers the brain to signal the body to increase production of a particular hormone. The feeling will depend on the hormone the body produces.

This is the component of anger studied by the researchers who concluded that aggressive boys do not have adequate levels of cortisol, a hormone often seen in fear. Some noted experts, reading the study's results, suggested that the lack of a fear sensation allows the young men to ignore fear cues in the environment. As a result, they do not fear the potential consequences of their aggressive behaviors.[7]

Although cortisol has been given the research spotlight recently, adrenaline is the primary hormone involved in fear or anger.[8] The additional supply of adrenaline, with its pain-numbing, energy-producing properties, makes possible the many positive functions of anger discussed in chapter 2. Without adrenaline, a person could still have an angry interpretation about an event, but the results would not be the same because there would be no angry feeling. The chemical properties of adrenaline make the emotion happen.

Emotion

The increased supply of a chemical creates a physiological sensation that the person recognizes and labels. The body responds to the hormone by creating the physiological sensation, which gives rise to the emotion. A sociological aspect exists along with this biophysiological phenomenon: The sensation needs to be named. Through socialization, people are taught the feeling labels used to name the emotion.

Behavior

The behavior component of the feeling process deals with how people choose to express their angry emotions. Once people label the emotion, they act according to what they have learned as an appropriate expression of that feeling in the given situation. The actions people take when expressing any emotion differ from person to person and depend on a number of factors. A major factor is whether that emotion was acceptable in the individual's family of origin. In homes where the emotion was acceptable, children have the opportunity to imitate how the adults express the feeling. Another major determinant of behavior that expresses a feeling is the number and types of experiences a person has had. Experiences offer potential modifications to the behaviors learned when younger and provide a wider array of options.

Behaviorists, such as Albert Bandura, have studied this piece of the process extensively. One of Bandura's studies done in the 1960s continues to influence how psychologists view people's behaviors.[9] In that study, he discovered that children who had viewed aggressive behaviors on film were likely to imitate those behaviors when in a similar life situation. More recently, other researchers have investigated whether Bandura's findings apply to watching aggression on TV. Their results indicate that adolescents who watch hours of violence on TV daily are more likely to commit acts of violence. Adolescents who watch less TV each day and who watch music or comedy shows are less likely to behave aggressively. These findings help to validate the idea that behaviors are learned through imitation.[10]

Because TV viewing is relatively passive, video games and Internet chat rooms may have even greater potential for eliciting aggression because the participants take an active role in the projected violence. Active participation requires more areas of the brain and body to be involved in the learning process, which results in learning the aggressive behaviors more quickly and with greater intensity.

Reaction

After the person chooses an action, other people near enough to notice the behavior react to it. A mother reacts to her six-year-old daughter with a frown and admonishment when the child begins eating the mashed potatoes with her fingers. A woman reacts to her fiancé's confession of philandering by pulling the engagement ring off her finger and throwing it at him. A manager responds to a worker's efforts with a smile, a handshake, and a thank-you. These reactions and the messages they are meant to convey are obvious to anyone watching the interchange. Some reactions and their meanings are more difficult to detect, however: the slight lift of an eyebrow, silence, a fake smile accompanied by platitudes.

If no one observes the behavior, or if the event is internal, the reaction happens in the person's own mind. Human beings do not need to have another living person present for the reaction component of the feeling process to take place. Often I have heard friends utter, "Oh, if my mother could see me now, she'd have a fit." They are imagining another person's reaction to their behaviors.

Reaction/Event

Whether apparent or surreptitious, external or internal, the socially adept person notices the reaction. At this point, the reaction has become another event that initiates the circular feeling process again:

- The person interprets the reaction/event. (The six-year-old girl knows her mother's frown means disapproval.)
- The brain tells the body to produce more of a chemical. (A slight amount of extra adrenaline is released into the six-year-old's system.)
- An internal sensation occurs and the person identifies it. (The girl recognizes the internal reaction as a danger signal.)
- The person chooses an action from an array of behavioral options and implements the behavior. (The girl remembers that the last time she ignored her mother's frown her mother smacked her hand, and so she picks up the fork to eat her potatoes.)
- Finally, anyone observing notices the behavior and responds to it. (The mother smiles and begins eating her dinner.)

The reaction is then an event and the process begins all over again.

Everyone Is Doing It

This process may seem cumbersome, time-consuming, or, at the very least, extremely complicated. The entire series of the components, however, usually plays out in a second or less and is so fluid and spontaneous that we are not aware of its complexity. For me, social situations become periods of wonderment when I remember that, during waking hours, this complex, circular process is happening within everyone, all the time. If I am having dinner with five other people, six emotional processes are influencing the social interactions throughout the evening. There is the possibility of six different interpretations for everything that is said or done, leading to a number of possible feelings and six different behavioral expressions for each of those feelings. Then there is the chance that each behavior will elicit five different reactions, which means that six separate events will occur at the same time. The possibilities grow exponentially.

Fortunately for our emotional equilibrium, most social interactions avoid chaos because people have common understandings and expectations in the context of social situations. This is one of the major outcomes of each culture's socialization process. People know how they are expected to act when sitting down to eat dinner. Because of the strong influence of socialization, feelings and their resultant behaviors must be viewed against the sociocultural background where they occur. When you keep the social context in mind, your response will be more effective. This is especially true when the emotion is anger because so many social dictates and restraints determine what expression of this common feeling is permissible.

ANGER AND THE FEELING PROCESS

In many respects, each component of the feeling process functions in a similar manner for all emotions. But because of the purpose that anger is meant to fulfill, there are a number of differences in the anger process.

The most basic purpose of the internal reaction associated with anger is to protect and defend ourselves against physical and emotional attacks. Because of this function, anger is designed to act in ways that are opposite of other feelings. Anger, as a protective device, pushes people away in order to create distance. Loneliness, in serving its function of gathering humans together for survival, pulls people closer. Anger demands that we stay and fight. Fear commands a fast getaway. These contradictory goals produce the confusion and misunderstandings associated with angry feelings. People, many professional counselors included, attempt to force anger to fit the same mold as other emotions.

This does not mean that the circular feeling process doesn't apply to anger. Anger's course through the process provides a means of clarifying confusing aspects of this common feeling, as long as the similarities and differences with other emotions are clearly delineated within each component.

Figure B (page 49), "Constructive Anger," shows how angry feelings can be used productively. This linear adaptation of the circular diagram in figure A is helpful in understanding the differences between anger and other emotions.

Emotion

The biggest difference between anger and other emotional sensations resides in the emotion area, so this piece of the process needs to be examined first. Unlike other feelings, anger is never a primary emotion. It never occurs alone. Anger is the child of fear and as such is always preceded by some form of fear. It might be anxiety, nervousness, or terror. The level or size of the fear is determined by the amount of adrenaline released into the body. If it is advantageous and possible for the person to leave the fear-producing situation, then the most effective action is for the body to maintain the fear and use the excessive adrenaline to flee. But if it is not advantageous to leave or there is no avenue of escape, the internal sensation created by the additional adrenaline is renamed as anger. With this new label, the body prepares to fight. This relabeling of the internal sensation happens so fast that we may not even realize that we originally felt afraid.

On the diagram, a dotted line crosses the Emotion area between fear and anger. Since anger is an emotion, it belongs in this area. Its protective function, though, requires building walls and creating distance. It masks another emotion, fear. Because anger defends, it can look more like a defense mechanism than a feeling.

When responding to an angry person, you must remember the subordinate relationship anger has to fear. If your goal is to reduce the anger in order to get beyond a conflict, encouraging the person to share or vent his angry feelings will do little if any good. When defenses are validated through repetition, they become stronger. As long as the person continues to feel afraid and perceives no escape, the defense is still necessary and the anger remains. Instead, if you want the anger reduced, you must respond in a manner that helps the person address the fear hidden beneath the angry feeling.

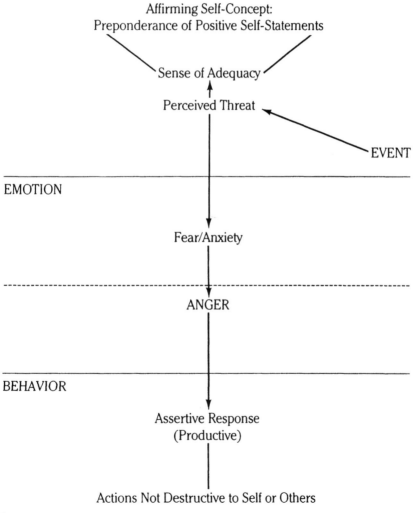

CONSTRUCTIVE ANGER

THOUGHT

Affirming Self-Concept:
Preponderance of Positive Self-Statements

Sense of Adequacy

Perceived Threat

EVENT

EMOTION

Fear/Anxiety

ANGER

BEHAVIOR

Assertive Response
(Productive)

Actions Not Destructive to Self or Others

Figure B

The concept that anger performs a defensive function does not negate the fact that it is an emotion. Anger involves a physiological response, which can be labeled, to an external event. It prepares the body to fight emotional and physical attacks. Its purpose is to defend. To try to make anger fit the mold of other feelings denies its very character and adds to the problems that people experience with it.

Revisiting the example of my cat from the beginning of this chapter shows how simple the process can be. If my cat had been cornered by the contractor, she would have arched her back and let loose a terrible hiss. Her fear would have turned to anger and she would be ready to fight. Her instinct to protect herself against a perceived danger would have instigated the transformation of fear to anger, a natural survival mechanism for a trapped animal.

Thought

Human beings, with their higher mental capabilities, not only have the same instinctive reaction as a cat to physical danger, they also respond to emotional and psychological threats using the fear-to-anger connection. The human neocortex allows individuals, using abstract ideas and symbols, to form a concept of self and to decide how that self interacts with the immediate environment and fits with the rest of the world.

Human beings at birth do not have a concept of self. Whether called self-concept, self-image, or self-identity, the idea of self as it relates to the rest of humanity begins developing shortly after birth. Imagine the infant's self-concept as a blank piece of paper. This page will not remain blank for very long. It will fill up with positive and negative evaluations as if significant people in the child's immediate surroundings were writing them down. When a child makes a mistake and her father calls her an idiot, the phrase "I am an idiot" is added to the sheet. The same process occurs with praise. If the child brings home a good report card and the father tells her how smart and good she is, the short evaluative statements "I am smart" and "I am good," are added to the self-concept paper.

From the beginning, the child internalizes the judgments bestowed by others as if they were her own creation. She will carry this imaginary piece of paper with her the rest of her life and believe the short evaluative sentences to be true, whether they are or not. With new experiences and achievements, new statements may be added that support or negate the original ones.

Eventually, the paper is filled. Statements overlap and hide others. Some can no longer be read clearly. The statements that stand out are those that were learned early in life because the paper was clean and they were easy to read. Also, statements written during traumatic events remain clear and strong because the emotional impact highlights them. From this imaginary page comes the basis for personal evaluation and personal identity. Because of that, all interpretations of external events are colored by the short evaluative statements on this paper.

When the page contains many more positive than negative statements, an affirming self-concept evolves. The person believes herself to be a worthy human being, one who deserves respect but does not ask to be worshipped. She is equal to others, neither above nor below the rest of humanity.

An affirming self-concept furnishes a sense of adequacy, a general overall feeling of being equipped to handle whatever life might bring. It allows the person to make a mistake without feeling the shame of self-degradation. An affirming self-concept produces a realistic perception of oneself and how one fits into the surrounding world.

Anger's role is to protect this sense of adequacy from events that are perceived as threats to the affirming self-concept. Because a person with an affirming self-concept views the world realistically, her interpretation of events in her life are usually accurate, meaning that she correctly assesses any threats made to her self-esteem. When she thinks she has been put down, probability is high that she has been put down and that the anger that she feels is appropriate.

Behavior

One afternoon in the spring of 1992, I turned the TV on to catch the latest news. The reporter was interviewing a woman in West Virginia whose story I will never forget because she carried her anger so beautifully. She was a mother of two children under the age of ten. She was divorced and, during the divorce proceedings, had lost her house to her ex-husband. She was angry about that and decided she would have a house that was totally hers, a house no one could ever take away. Working as a waitress, she saved enough money to buy land. She continued working and saved enough money for the foundation's concrete. She poured it herself. She worked some more and saved more and bought the lumber for the frame. She checked out books from the library and talked to contractors about framing. When she was ready, that house frame went up by her hands. The only other help came from her young children. She repeated this process with every aspect of the house. At the time of the newscast, the process had been going on for about eight years. At that point the shell was up, there was a roof, and it was obvious that her craftsmanship was close to flawless. She estimated that it would take about five more years before the house was completed. I have no doubt that she completed that house and that it is beautiful.

This woman's behavior demonstrated the quintessence of constructive anger. She used the motivation provided by this high-energy emotion to produce what she and her family needed without depriving other people of their needs. Her anger built rather than destroyed.

WHO IS RESPONSIBLE FOR WHAT

Anger expressed in as healthy a manner usually requires the simplest of responses. In a strong, enthusiastic voice, I would respond to the anger of the woman in the story above with, "You go, woman! Can I help carry the lumber?" Responding to constructive anger is simple because it is clean. Its expression is not muddied by blaming someone else, wallowing in self-pity, or waiting for the world to change so you can be happy again. The angry person takes responsibility for her components of the feeling process, while the responder recognizes that and only takes responsibility for his part of that process.

When two people have an angry encounter, neither, both, or either person may be responsible for the event that initiates the feeling process. From the moment the triggering event is over, who is responsible for what component of the feeling process is clear-cut. The angry individual is responsible for the thought, emotion, and behavior areas. The person responding to that anger is accountable for only one piece of the process—the reaction.

Accurate allocation of responsibility is the base for developing effective responses to another person's anger. When relating to another person, you are responsible only for your reaction to that person's behavior. No one has the god-like power to reach in and change another person's interpretation of a situation—especially since that interpretation is the product of a self-identity that took years to create.

No one makes anyone else feel angry. Anger is an internal, chemical reaction that the person has learned to label. It is his reaction. It is his label. And how he behaves once that sensation is labeled remains his decision. Your only choice is how to react to it. The reaction you choose may take into account and influence the angry person's feeling components, as we will see in chapter 6. But to change any other components remains the responsibility of the person experiencing them. Emotionally healthy people intuitively know this and respond accordingly.

Implementing your chosen reaction produces a new event for the angry person's feeling circle to process. Everything from your initial reaction (turned new event) until the process reaches the reaction again becomes the angry individual's responsibility.

Throughout this chapter we have seen how emotions, specifically anger, were designed to function. But what happens when the components do not function as expected?

4

Problems That Can
Occur with Anger

WHEN WE RESPOND TO SOMEONE'S ANGER, we bring our personal feelings into the interaction. How we and the other person experience the components of this personalized emotional process determines whether the anger is lessened or intensified, whether it is constructive or destructive, whether it is useful or abusive.

The difficulty of obtaining a positive outcome from an angry interchange becomes apparent when we consider the number of factors that must operate together with a minimum number of flaws. Each person enters the interaction responsible for five components, excluding the external event (Thought, Chemical, Emotion, Behavior, Reaction). If two people are engaged, then ten components are involved. Because the process is circular, a distortion or malfunction in one component can adversely affect the nine other components.

When we look at the process in this way, the odds of manufacturing a positive outcome to the interchange dwindle. These odds become even lower as the interchange continues. Again, because of the circular nature of the process, the negative effect on each of the variables increases dramatically and rapidly with each turn through the circle. A flaw in one component distorts the next component, which distorts the next, which distorts the next, until the circle brings all the distortions back to the original flaw, which is only validated and exaggerated by the process.

For example, one morning Jack expressed his anger at work aggressively and people reacted by avoiding him. He interpreted their behavior as meaning "They do not like me," a psychologically threatening interpretation. His brain released adrenaline. Because he had to continue working, he felt trapped and his anxiety turned to anger. When someone approached him with work-related questions, he snapped and replied with cutting sarcasm. Co-workers avoided him more. As his interpretation was validated again and again by their reactions, his behavior became more and more aggressive. Once such an unhealthy cycle is started, the potential to continue it is great. But at any time, anyone can respond to another's anger in a way that offers a healthy alternative.

DISTORTIONS WITHIN EACH COMPONENT

Human beings are social animals. Very few people live in isolation, and even people who tend to seek seclusion were raised by and lived with significant others for periods in their lives. The effects of social interactions, no matter how brief, upon a person's inner life cannot be overestimated. People learn and transmit cultural norms through social groups (family, church, school, friends, and others) that adapt and reject the larger society's patterns, customs, and beliefs, depending upon their specific needs. Social instruction begins before an infant can talk and continues until death, imparting cultural knowledge through both subtle and obvious methods. This kind of teaching is so pervasive that the lessons are internalized without most people being aware of the instruction.

Cultural training can be so potent that people accept its lessons as absolute truths to be personalized and used for self-evaluation. Cultural training, through parental instruction, teaches children the labels for their feelings and shapes their behavior. In fact, culture impacts every aspect of a person's emotions. It enters the emotional process through the Reaction area of the feeling circle. Therefore, even though the person responding to someone else's anger has responsibility for only one variable—the Reaction component—the possibilities for influencing the angry person's other emotional factors are numerous. To use this powerful component most effectively, the responder needs to understand the distortions that may be occurring within the other components. The responder then has a greater opportunity to ameliorate rather than exacerbate the problem component's flaws.

Figure C shows how each area of constructive anger can be distorted to produce destructive anger.

DESTRUCTIVE ANGER

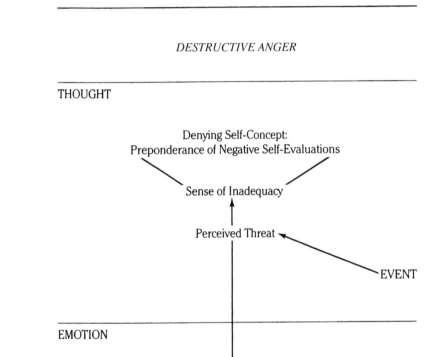

THOUGHT

Denying Self-Concept:
Preponderance of Negative Self-Evaluations

Sense of Inadequacy

Perceived Threat

EVENT

EMOTION

Fear/Anxiety

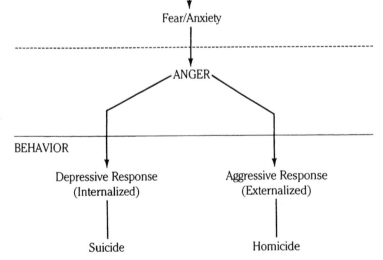

ANGER

BEHAVIOR

Depressive Response
(Internalized)

Aggressive Response
(Externalized)

Suicide

Homicide

Figure C

Thought

I would estimate that a large percentage of all unnecessary anger arousal is initiated by misinterpreted events, leading to poor communication. The majority of problematic anger occurs because the Thought component of the feeling process does not function as smoothly as it could. Because all interpretations are filtered through self-concept, the inability to accurately perceive reality is connected to how an individual perceives himself or herself. This misperception distorts the event and any communications inherent within the event.

As described in chapter 3, self-perception is dictated by one's self-evaluative statements. Some of these are positive, "I'm good," and some are negative, "I'm bad." Trauma almost always adds negative self-statements to one's self-concept, especially when it occurs during childhood. Young children, thinking that they are the center of the universe, internalize environmental events as part of themselves. Children who are harshly punished for making a small error in judgment do not think, "I made a mistake." They internalize the situation as "I am a mistake." Negative self-evaluations consist of short judgmental statements such as "I'm stupid," "I am not important," "I'm worthless," "I'm not good enough," and "I'm wrong." Negative self-statements can be contained in even more hurtful declarations such as "I'm a freak," "I'm awful," "I'm a monster."

Negative self-statements can also be acquired from less noticeable events. A common example is the subtle development of the evaluation "I'm not important." When family dynamics do not provide a forum for children to express feelings about family decisions, especially those that have a direct effect on the children, youngsters start to think, "If I were important, they'd care." When the family continues to neglect a child's opinions and feelings, that thought becomes internalized as "I'm not important."

People who collect more negative than positive judgments of their character and personality develop a self-concept that revolves around denying their worthiness. A strong sense of inadequacy develops. This doesn't mean they think they are inadequate to perform some task. It is much deeper than that. They believe they are inadequate as a human being; something inside of them is defective. They interpret daily events through this sense of inadequacy and the many concurrent negative self-statements that continually feed it.

When Betty's supervisor walks by her, deep in thought, and neglects to say, "Good morning," Betty's self-statement "I'm not important" interprets the event as though Betty is being ignored because she lacks importance. Her esteem is threatened. A low-level sensation of fear begins. Her thoughts jump to, "How rude. Who does he think he is?" And the fear changes to anger.

The irony is that the negative self-statements that generate the hurtful perceptions are lies. Making a mistake does not mean that a person is a mistake as a human being. One person's feelings are not more or less important than another's. It is false to believe that someone's humanity is so flawed that that person is internally defective.

People who pass through life perceiving the day's events, especially the behavior of people close to them, from this type of hurtful perspective are very defensive. Co-workers, acquaintances, even family members begin staying away. Others' avoidance validates the negative self-statements, making them stronger and more powerful.

When you respond to someone whose anger is initiated by misperceived events based on negative self-statements, it is helpful to know that avoidance escalates anger. Ignoring the person who is angry, changing the subject, turning your back, or walking away bolsters the negative self-statements that triggered the initial anger and intensify the angry feelings.

Another perceptual problem that can distort the Thought component involves cultural context. Word meanings, tonal nuances, facial expressions, and hand gestures provide social clues for deciphering personal encounters. Someone who attempts to interact with people from a culture whose customs are unfamiliar may inadvertently perform some extreme blunders of etiquette. Such *faux pas* are often misinterpreted as rudeness rather than a lack of cultural awareness.

Emotion

A man in his early twenties was referred to me for counseling by his probation officer for his explosively angry outbursts. The most recent incident ended when he punched his hand through a wall. During our first interview, I asked him if he wanted to change what was happening with his anger. Without hesitation, he said, "No."

His response shocked me for a moment because this was the first time I had ever had anyone answer that way. Usually people who have lost control of angry impulses realize that the people close to them are being hurt. After an emotional explosion, they feel a great deal of remorse and may even vow to never do it again. Without knowing how to change their anger response, it does happen again. They are trapped. Help in obtaining freedom is usually welcomed by answering the question I posed to this young man with a strong yes.

My curiosity quickly recovered my presence of mind, and I asked what his answer was all about. He replied, "I like the way it feels." This young man had discovered something that most people do not realize: The physiological sensation of anger can be enjoyable. Angry feelings are created by a chemical/hormonal surge. Extra adrenaline is going through the body. It is an energizing, motivating force. The body's internal reaction is very similar to the one produced during exciting, adventurous experiences such as skydiving or competitive sports. The difference is that the internal sensation incurred during those activities is socially sanctioned. Participants are supposed to feel that way and the experience is supposed to be pleasurable.

But socially supported misinformation teaches that anger is bad, and therefore you are not supposed to feel it. And if it does occur, it is a bad, unpleasant feeling to have. Because it is human nature to abstain from situations that cause discomfort, many people have been socialized that anger needs to be avoided.

The idea that anger should be avoided leads to a number of problems in the Emotion component. Most of these problems arise from mislabeling the internal sensation. Some people do this by naming the feeling arousal with words or phrases that are not emotional labels, such as "I'm bored with X," "I'm tired of Y," "I'm disappointed in Z." These phrases describe judgments or physiological sensations other than those deemed emotional, and, therefore, allow people to avoid acknowledging the sensation as anger.

A similar anger-avoidance technique is to use verb forms as names for the internal arousal. "I feel distanced," "I feel left out," and "I feel betrayed" demonstrate ways people elude their own anger by labeling internal sensations with passive verb forms. This method is very clever because not only is the anger sensation avoided, but many people are duped into believing that they are sharing their feelings in an assertive way. *Distanced, left out,* and *betrayed* are not feelings. They do not name an internal, physiological sensation. And just because someone places the word *feel* in front of these words does not make them into emotions. They are passive forms of verbs that describe what the angry individual *perceives* someone to be doing to him. Accuracy would be better served if the person rephrased these statements to "I think I was distanced," "I think I was left out," "I think I was betrayed." The emotion that results from these perceptions often is anger. But it does not have to be. It could be happiness, depending upon what the person is being distanced from or left out of.

When someone uses words to avoid stating the actual feeling, there is an element of victimization in that person's perception of what is happening. "I feel left out" implies that someone left someone out. The someone left out was *me,* and *you* are the one who did the leaving out. This is not assertiveness. This is accusation disguised as assertiveness.

If you are having a verbal exchange with someone using these methods to avoid personal anger, remember that the internal sensation normally labeled anger is there, but it is being called by another name. Special care needs to be taken when interacting with a person who replaces feelings with verbs. The responder in this situation may lose effectiveness by falling into the trap of defending against the implied accusation rather than responding to the anger.

Another common technique to avoid anger is to deny that it exists. It is important to remember that this technique is not only designed to deceive other people. It also fools the person who is angry. The person's mind actually convinces itself that the physiological sensation occurring within the body is not anger. Usually this technique is expressed in a very straightforward manner. When I ask the person if she is angry, she responds, "No." Another very common reply is: "No. Why get angry? It won't change anything." A person who makes this type of statement is very angry. The phrase "It won't change anything" sends the message that something hurtful is going on, I know it, and I cannot do anything about it. This statement is the posture of a victim. Anger is a common emotion experienced by all victimized individuals, even when the victimization is perceived rather than real.[1] It is also the most common emotion that victimized people avoid by denying.

Actively avoiding anger is a distortion of the Emotion component that is the opposite of what my young, angry client did. He felt angry more often than most people and knew it. He grew up in a home where the only emotional expression he witnessed was anger. That was the limit of his feeling knowledge, and so he tended to tag all internal sensations as anger. When others would be expressing sadness, he showed an angry response. Even when the situation clearly called for an expression of happiness, he displayed anger.

The young male client was demonstrating an exaggeration of another common problem that develops in the Emotion component of the feeling process—the mislabeling of fear as anger. If you know someone who says, "I never feel afraid," you know someone who avoids fear by calling it anger. This is very common in our Clint Eastwood, make-my-day society.

Researcher Norma Feshbach, while working with children, discovered that six-year-olds could label the basic feelings of mad, glad, sad, and afraid.[2] Girls had few problems naming any of their internal reactions. Boys had difficulties with only one of the labels, fear. In our culture, a vast majority of males before the age of six have been socialized to believe that it is not acceptable to feel afraid. Our bodies are set up in such a way that denied fear becomes anger. Many of the males socialized to dismiss fear as unmanly transform their fear to anger and appear to have an overabundance of angry feelings.

Besides the problems generated by the culturally induced mislabeling of internal sensations, the healthy functioning of the Emotion component can be disrupted by disturbances in the body's chemical makeup. A person's emotions are dependent on the levels of the chemicals present within the body. Bipolar disorder and schizophrenia are serious illnesses that demonstrate the impact a chemical imbalance can have on a person's feeling life. Alcohol and other central nervous system depressant drugs can relax a nervous person by changing his or her chemical makeup. Cocaine initiates a euphoric rush that, with the slightest affront, can quickly turn to anger. Steroids may make a person anxious and easily irritable. Psychiatrists prescribe Prozac to alleviate depression. Paxil relieves panic attacks. Caffeine helps energize, while milk assists with sleep. All of the described mood changes are chemically induced.

The impact of chemicals on a person's emotional reaction is so profound that I will not attempt to counsel someone who is high or drunk. Anything I say is likely to be overridden by the chemical effects of the drug.

Also, I do very limited counseling with people who are going through the detoxification process. Throughout an addicted person's extensive use of drugs, the body has attempted to mobilize its natural chemicals to counteract the drugs' effects. The human body will continue to do this during detoxification, creating unnaturally low lows, high levels of anxiety, and extreme irritability. Time, more than talking, will improve these extensive mood swings. In fact, in most instances where anger is created through purely chemical imbalances, the best interventions are time and counteractive chemicals.

Another way the body's chemistry affects the recognition and identification of emotions involves hormonal production through exercise, especially weightlifting. I have not been able to find any studies that validate or negate my opinions in this area, but in my twenty-five years of counseling, I have noticed that my clients who lift weights on a regular schedule take longer than nonlifters to realize that they are having an internal reaction that indicates anger arousal. When I first became aware of this phenomenon, I began asking the weightlifters if they understood that they were involved in provocative instances in their lives for an inordinately long time before feeling angry. Each one indicated he was not aware of the internal reaction early in the anger experience. They did not know there was a feeling sensation going on. The more I talk with weightlifters, the more I am convinced that the hormones and the physiological arousal produced by lifting weights so closely resemble the anger chemistry and internal reaction that the weightlifters, having experienced the chemical effects often, are desensitized to them. This creates the need for greater amounts of adrenaline or a longer time for the weightlifter to notice the resultant sensation.

Behavior

The actions people employ to express anger depend on how their Emotion component functions and on the quantity and types of angry behaviors they've witnessed throughout their lives. Generally, someone whose Emotion component allows an awareness of anger sensations and whose personal history presents aggression as a viable problem-solving tool tends to use an aggressive response style. This style always involves some form of attack directed outward, usually toward someone else. This person is angry, knows it, and targets another person to blame for it. There are a number of ways that blame can be expressed, including verbal put-downs, sarcasm, and physical assault, even homicide. People around this person feel the onslaught of the attack or, if they are not the target of the ire, they are aware they are witnessing an incident of psychic battering. They know the person is angry. After the outburst, the victim and witnesses might review the aggressive episode. They probably describe the angry individual as hostile, arrogant, belligerent, viperous, or any number of other equally negative adjectives. The anger underneath the behaviors will be described in much the same way, because the aggressive response style involves behaviors that hurt others and that clearly indicate anger as the triggering emotion.

When a person continually expresses angry emotions aggressively, the negative adjectives applied to the behaviors and to the emotion will be used to describe the person. In fact, the aggressor most likely internalized those adjectives long ago. After every aggressive episode, the hurtful adjectives are reactivated and not only affirm but exacerbate the person's negative self-statements.

The Behavior component of constructive anger alters differently when angry feelings are avoided rather than identified in the Emotion component. People who avoid anger develop a depressive response style. Their behaviors help them sustain their avoidance of the internal sensation that would be labeled anger if recognized. The actions they employ to disguise the feeling of anger can range from affable, such as joking and agreeing, to unpleasant expressions of self-pity, pouting, and whining.

Because the public behaviors contradict what is happening internally, anyone attempting to respond to a person employing the depressive response style may become very confused. In social situations, when one person is joking and laughing, etiquette calls for others to laugh along with the individual. When the jokester is internalizing anger, the discomfort that something is not quite right impinges on others' enjoyment of the laughter. The responder, seeing the tightness around the person's jaw and tension around the eyes, realizes that the laughter is not an outcome of happiness but of something else.

Some angry people use self-pity to mask the anger. It is common to feel sad and want to cry when in the presence of someone whose sadness is so great that it produces tears. But when tears of self-pity roll down someone's cheeks, others nearby do not feel sad and want to cry also. In fact, they may experience a sensation of anger, leaving them confused about their emotional reaction. They may wonder if something is wrong with them. When someone close by is crying, isn't it socially understood that we will be empathetic and experience sadness also? Instead, we have the urge to respond aggressively. If you find yourself in a situation like this and your emotional reaction is similar, there is a high probability that you *are* being empathetic. Empathy is being sensitive to and vicariously experiencing the feelings and thoughts of another. Under the tears of self-pity lies the internal sensation of anger, and that is the emotion you are empathetically reacting to. When interacting with a person who generally uses a depressive response style, do not pay as much attention to your eyes or ears as you pay to your emotions. I am convinced that one person's emotions respond accurately to another's dominant feeling state 90 percent of the time. And in the other 10 percent of the cases, it is not that the responder's feelings are off the mark but, more likely, that the other person is denying or misreading his or her internal sensations.

I have done hundreds of workshops designed to train business professionals on how to respond to other people's anger. Invariably, at each workshop, a participant asks me, "Why is it necessary to spend so much time identifying those who use a depressive response style? It is the aggressive workers that I supervise, or the aggressive customers that I deal with, that concern me and that I want to learn how to handle." Supervisors and managers need to be aware of workers whose response style is depressive because very few people use one response style exclusively. People tend to jump from one style to another. When this happens with workers whose dominant style is depressive, they may be secretively aggressive by sabotaging work efforts. The young man in chapter 1 who urinated in the ice cream is an example of an employee using the depressive response in the boss's presence and, when safely out of view, changing to an aggressive style. The supervisor may not have wanted to spend the time recognizing this young man's anger, but I am sure the customers, had they known of the resultant behavior, would have greatly appreciated it.

The intimidation wielded by an angry and aggressive customer is obviously unpleasant and time-consuming. It puts pressure on workers, interferes with tasks, and disrupts the business's emotional environment. Neglecting the less evident anger hidden beneath the depressive response style of a dissatisfied customer can result in equal unpleasantness and time consumption. I have lost track of the number of times a frustrated worker has mumbled, just loud enough for me to hear: "I have bent over backward to help this customer, and he keeps on whining. Nothing seems to satisfy him." Asking "why?" is another depressive ploy customers implement unintentionally to mask anger. It can be excessively time-consuming. Recently I was seduced for twenty minutes by a client's father who repeatedly asked me "why" questions about his insurance and our fee schedule before it occurred to me that the man was not really looking for information. He was attempting to deal with the internal sensation instigated by his insurance company's refusal to provide full coverage for our services. Once I responded to the anger underneath the "why" questions, the conversation changed quickly and we could move on to other issues.

The way a person expresses anger is not solely dependent on how the Emotion component is skewed. Another enormously influential factor is socialization. A six-year-old boy stands in a school in Mount Morris Township, Michigan, pointing a revolver at another boy. Without a word, he deftly swings the gun away from the lad, aims it at a six-year-old girl, and pulls the trigger. A few days later on the Sunday morning talk show "This Week," the four regular high-powered political analysts used the incident to discuss whether this would stir Congress into passing a new, supposedly tougher, gun control law.[3] George Will repeatedly attempted to interrupt his colleagues' discussion by vehemently stating, "Stop. You are missing the issue. The problem is not with guns. It is with the disintegration of the family."

On the contrary, valid research indicates that weapon carrying and discharge by youth is not influenced by the family's level of intactness. The strongest variable is the attitude about violence that caretakers convey to the youth.[4] The six-year-old who pulled the trigger lived in an environment where guns were accepted. He found it loaded, under his uncle's pillow. The child had most likely witnessed his uncle handling the gun, possibly even flaunting it by enacting the move used by the boy to shoot the girl. The youngster did what was developmentally expected of him. He mimicked the behavior of an adult.

Mr. Will's contention that guns are not the problem is a hair's width away from being fallacious. Society's acceptance of guns and what they symbolize is the problem. A culture that says it is all right for individuals to possess weapons capable of lethal destruction is a culture that condones violence. The United States is such a culture. Violence is a learned behavior. The youngster who fired at his schoolmate was amply socialized to perform that violent behavior. He saw it on the streets near his home, on television, as a national response to other governments, in school, and as a part of video games. Again, he did what was developmentally expected. He acted out the behaviors society had taught him.

Although the discussion has focused on aggressive behaviors as a product of socialization, depressive styles of responding are also culturally induced. Recently I had a client, an adolescent female, who showed up for an appointment with surface cut marks on her arms. When I asked about them, she replied, "Well, Tammy told me that she relieves emotional pain by cutting herself. I thought I'd try it and see if it worked." This young woman had entered a subculture where self-mutilation, perhaps not encouraged, was at least acceptable enough to be discussed as a viable way to reduce emotional pain. Her social network taught her a new behavior.

DESTRUCTIVE INTERACTIONS

Unhealthy expressions of angry feelings commonly elicit a nonconstructive response. Figure D (page 67) illustrates the process that creates destructive inter-personal communications when one angry person with distorted components of the feeling circle interacts with another person who has skewed components. The result is an increase in both participants' destructive anger.

The process begins with one person interpreting an event as threatening. Additional adrenaline is produced and labeled as fear. The fear changes to anger and is expressed in either a depressive or aggressive response style. This expression is accurately perceived as threatening by the other person. In fact, the perceived threat will be amplified if the destructive style triggers a conditioned emotional reaction. For example, if the person who is responding to anger has learned to expect punishment when someone is angry, then that person's emotional reaction is likely to be disproportionate to the situation. This being the case, whether that person responds with a depressive style by using withdrawal or placating behaviors, or with an aggressive style by employing attacking or combative behaviors, the chosen response will be destructive and out of proportion to the expressed anger. That person's response becomes another event that the first person interprets as a threat. The process continues and both people's anger distortions grow with each pass through the process.

I witness this process every day, many times a day. It happens between strangers in grocery stores, between lovers, between close friends, between

DESTRUCTIVE INTERACTIONS

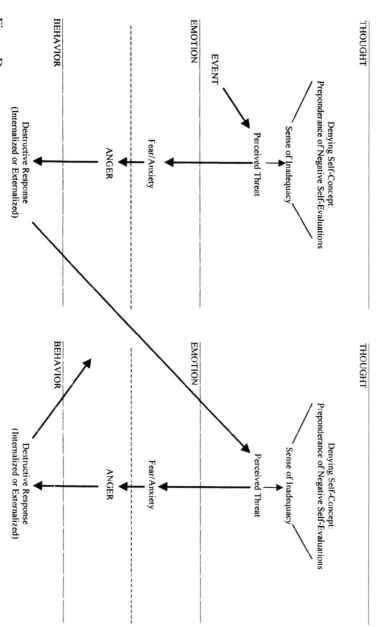

Figure D

business associates, between employees and supervisors, and on and on and on. A clear and powerful demonstration of this process occurs in the highly publicized phenomenon of road rage. A man, let's call him Mr. Smith, begins his annual vacation. He is relaxed while driving 65 to 70 miles an hour on Route 95. All of a sudden a little red Fiat convertible goes zooming by, makes a sharp cut into his lane just ahead of his front bumper, and keeps on going. Mr. Smith tightens, takes a quick draw of breath, and hits his brakes. His safety was threatened. The adrenaline flowed. The physiological response triggered fear. He reacted by hitting his brakes. Mr. Smith is not hurt. He is now safe. To this point, the process has been instinctive and constructive. The person in the red Fiat blithely goes on, probably unaware of the discomfort caused by her careless driving.

There is no need for Mr. Smith's fear to change to anger for protection. An emotionally healthy person recognizes the fear, is grateful that no harm occurred, and takes a deep breath to help his body reduce the adrenaline. But in Mr. Smith, a negative self-statement from his neocortex has been triggered. The statement activated can be either closely or transiently connected to the actual incident. He may have a self-evaluation such as "I'm worthless." Being physically threatened triggers this statement, which was probably created during childhood physical abuse. If this is the case, physical threat and worthlessness have been conditioned to occur together. Instead of taking a deep breath to help his body reduce the anger-inducing adrenaline, Mr. Smith externalizes the angry feelings with the idea "Who the hell does she think she is!" This conscious thought, by focusing his attention outward, serves to hide the hurtful self-evaluation. Now the situation with the Fiat is construed as a personal affront. Mr. Smith, in control of a powerful two-ton weapon, hits the gas pedal to catch up with the red convertible. Once there, he will unnecessarily use that weapon as a violent means to protect his self-esteem.

The outcome of the altercation depends heavily on how the driver of the Fiat responds. If the Fiat driver has an affirming self-concept and can somehow indicate that she was in the wrong (in this example, she *was* in the wrong, even though cutting Mr. Smith off was inadvertent), Mr. Smith's rage will diminish.

Unfortunately, there is a high probability that a distortion has occurred in the Thought, Emotion, or Behavior components of anyone responding to another person's anger. The driver of the red car might have a negative self-statement that makes her interpret events through a denying self-concept that indicates, "I am wrong." If this is true, she is incapable of admitting to a serious mistake and has a strong need to defend herself. Or the person behind the steering wheel of the Fiat may be a street-tough person who is unable to identify feelings of fear. Very quickly her fears turn to anger. The dangerousness of the situation eludes her. She must fight back and she also has a two-ton weapon for her counterattack. Even the weakest human being has a sense of power when in control of an automobile. If the Fiat driver responds with any type of destructive behavior, whether an aggressive act such as attacking back or a depressive expression such as ignoring the angry driver, Mr. Smith's anger is likely to escalate to a dangerous level of rage.

Road rage is a swift and strong anger arousal. This extreme example of anger escalation combines the instinct-initiated anger of potential physical danger and anger generated by the neocortex as it perceives an emotional threat. Usual daily encounters with another person's anger involve less intense and dangerous interactions. In fact, they can begin with an innocuous phrase interpreted incorrectly. With no immediately apparent life-threatening harm, the responder has the time to react in a manner that will move the interchange in a positive direction. Unfortunately, the ingredients needed to redirect the interaction can be negatively affected by the person's historic exposure to anger, especially when the exposing incidents were traumatically induced during childhood.

Remember, what is traumatic for a child may be far less important to an adult. If the impetus for a response originates from childhood trauma, the person responds as though the other person's expressed anger is harmful and physically threatening. The responder perceives the other person's anger as a terrible and personal accusation. This emotional reaction is quick and founded upon an exaggerated fear, created during the childhood trauma, that conditioned her to expect a hurt-producing punishment. Her body does what it is supposed to do during threatening situations—it prepares to run/avoid/withdraw or to fight/attack/protect. These destructive behaviors produce a new event for the first person to interpret.

The process continues to generate destructive behavioral styles from each participant, increasing the responding person's fear of anger and heightening her inability to react effectively. In this way, what may have started as a minor misunderstanding between two people quickly evolves into a major altercation.

5

The Foundation

THE PREVIOUS CHAPTER DEMONSTRATED how two people, each with limited skills for expressing and responding to anger, exacerbate each others' deficiencies until they seem to have few behavioral alternatives remaining. Brawling, departing, and even less extreme responses to anger usually fail to produce a beneficial result.

Unfortunately, for many people these types of behaviors may be all they know and therefore all that they can expect. Or perhaps they know of other outcomes from their personal history but their internal reactions prevent them from achieving such outcomes. I have met people who immediately develop a defensive posture when encountering another's anger, even when that anger is leveled in an assertive, nondestructive manner. Just the tone of voice from a displeased supervisor or the cold stare from an angry mate could trigger an instinctive protective response. This response can be so strong that their breathing becomes shallow and their mind stops processing the incident.

If you have a similar response, then knowing what techniques can help you attain your goal when responding to another's anger is not enough. If you cannot implement them because of your personal physiological reaction, the techniques are of no use. Or, if you are unable to calm the inner voice of your negative self-statements in order to assess environmental cues, you may put yourself in dangerous situations, respond to inaccurate perceptions, or heighten the other person's anger by your body tension. Perhaps you find that other people become angry with you even when you are trying to help them. Then, the more you attempt to explain, the angrier they seem to get. Maybe the problem is not what you are attempting to say but the words you are using to say it. If any of these situations are familiar to you, it may be that you have not acquired certain types of necessary physiological, cognitive, and behavioral preparation.

Whatever your goal—whether it is to respond to your spouse's ire in a way that will increase intimacy, to defuse a customer's angry outburst efficiently, or to interact more positively with your angry child—the skills and techniques designed to produce your desired result are most effective when built upon a foundation of principled guidelines. In fact, you may discover that practicing the following guidelines will not only prepare you to implement the anger response skills discussed later on, but they will also reduce the number of angry encounters you experience. You will have fewer angry people around you in need of a response. As you read through these guidelines, you will find that a number of them have exercises to help you achieve the principle embodied within the guideline.

I. PUT SAFETY FIRST

Always put your safety and your children's safety first. If you encounter anger in a person who has a history of acting out angry feelings in violent, physically harmful ways and you have any hint that it is about to happen again, leave. You may have many reasons why you think you cannot leave, but this is a time when you need to mobilize your anger to perform its protective function. Use your angry feelings to develop a safety plan:

1. Locate public agencies that provide assistance and shelter.
2. If necessary, enlist friends and family for financial and emotional support.
3. Plan a safe means for physically leaving the premises.
4. Follow through by going to a safe place.

The skills described in this book are not therapeutic techniques. The ragefully violent person needs therapy; without it, the number of aggressive episodes increases and the level of violence escalates.

In my personal life, I avoid developing close relationships with people who I know are prone to violent outbursts, whether their violence is exhibited physically or emotionally. No one, not me or anyone else, deserves to experience the pain of physical abuse or the hurtful effects of verbal and emotional abuse. When I have erred in my initial judgment of someone's tendency to violence, later discovering that I have become a target for aggression, I have had to back away from that relationship and retreat into those relationships I know are safe. In some instances, this was emotionally difficult to do. But the result is a cadre of friends and loved ones who are kind people. Their kindness and benevolence encourages me to develop and maintain the same characteristics. This does not mean that we do not feel angry with each other's behavior, nor does it mean that we do not express our anger. It does mean, however, that anger is expressed and responded to in ways that are not physically hurtful or emotionally abusive. It also means that my circle of friends and my family members know that safety is a strong aspect in each of the relationships. This provides a platform of trust that makes responding to anger very easy because the fear of hurtful repercussion is not there to inhibit the response.

I am often asked, "What if it is my child who is physically or verbally abusive to me?" Family therapist Larry Fritzlan addressed this in an article titled "Raising the Bottom."[1] Although this article is about teenagers who are substance abusers, the principles it outlines can be used to help aggressive youth also. One of the principles—set limits and allow children to experience the consequences of their behavior—is a strong directive at the adolescent program where I work. It is important that the consequences are not capricious and arbitrary. They need to be real. In our culture, an adult hitting another adult is considered an assault, and the police are called. We do the same thing with adolescents. Once the adolescent is in police custody, parents and guardians have safe options to choose from. Most court systems, departments of social services, and mental health agencies have programs to assist with violent youth. Some of these programs are residential, placing aggressive children in a structured environment until they can demonstrate that they can express anger without hurting themselves or others.

2. THERE ARE NO GUARANTEES

I was discussing with my physician what life-saving procedures I might be comfortable having performed on me in an emergency. One of my main concerns was that I did not want brain damage. Her response stunned me.

She began by explaining that excessive blood loss or deprivation of oxygen to the brain often occurs in emergency situations. She ended by stating, "Therefore, in any medical emergency, I cannot guarantee that there will be no brain damage." If there are no guarantees in medicine, a science with physical applications, then there are even fewer guarantees when behavioral interventions are applied in response to a person's emotional being.

Human beings can be very fickle animals. They may choose one behavior over another at any given time, to any specific stimulus. When it comes to the efficacy of the skills and techniques I describe in this book, know that there are no guarantees. I am obliged to say to you the exact same thing that my doctor went on to say to me. I can only give you likelihood and probabilities.

There are two probabilities that I can give you right away. First, if you learn the response skills and techniques delineated in this book, you will have more options and a much higher probability of attaining your goal. Second, if you build a foundation today, using just what is in this chapter, you will like yourself more than you did yesterday and have a more pleasant tomorrow.

3. REDUCE THE CONDITIONED EMOTIONAL REACTION

If change were easy, we would all successfully mold ourselves to fulfill our personalized ideas of perfection. As anyone who has tried to remove a longstanding habit would attest, change can be difficult, emotionally unsettling work that sometimes requires guidance and assistance. Your ability to exchange the way you currently respond to other people's anger with a more effective behavior can be stymied by one of the most powerful instincts, that which warns of danger. If you have been conditioned to believe that physical or emotional harm follows another person's anger, then the internal reaction that you experience when facing that anger is very deep and possibly instinctive. This reaction was learned as a young child and has been reinforced by inaccurate thoughts and expectations of behavioral outcomes throughout life.

An instinctive response is extremely difficult to change. Whenever you are in the presence of angry feelings, your danger signal alerts your body that a threat to safety has occurred. As far as I know, there is no way to disconnect this signal. However, you can learn how to control your body's physiological and mental reactions to the signal. You accomplish this by using the relaxation technique below. Relaxation, combined with self-talk,[2] can direct the body to counteract the adrenaline.

Many of the exercises in this chapter and those throughout the book require relaxation and either self-talk or visualizations. Although not essential, a tape recorder and a relaxation tape may be beneficial. Relaxation tapes can be purchased from any major bookstore. Try to find one no longer than ten minutes. The short time frame limits the impact to a busy schedule and your mind will more likely remain focused for ten minutes than it will for twenty. I also recommend a tape that talks you through a relaxation exercise rather than just providing relaxing sounds.

If you do not have a relaxation tape, these steps are a way to relax:

1. Take a deep breath; hold it to the count of three.
2. Slowly let it out while thinking RELAX.
3. Take another deep breath; hold it to the count of three.
4. Slowly let it out while thinking RELAX.
5. Tighten both fists; count to three.
6. Open your fists and RELAX.
7. Take another deep breath; hold it to the count of three.
8. Slowly let it out while thinking RELAX.

Each day for three days find a time and a place where you can practice the relaxation technique that you have chosen. This will help you become more adept at using the skill of relaxation before applying it to other situations. After the three days of practice, when you are familiar with the sensation of being relaxed, try the following exercise.

Interrupting the Defensive Thought

It is counterproductive to have a thought that places you in a defensive mode while attempting to achieve a relaxed attitude. Therefore, this exercise is designed to interrupt defensive thoughts and to counteract the effects of increased adrenaline.

Before you start the exercise, hear yourself saying, in a strong firm tone, the word STOP. Now, say it again and again until the sound is clear and familiar.

Return to chapter 1 (pages 13–14) and choose a current angry episode:

What thoughts and feelings occurred during this incident?

In your usual place of relaxation, sitting in your usual comfortable position, close your eyes and start do the relaxation exercise that you have practiced. When you are relaxed:

- Visualize the angry episode that you chose.
- As soon as the thoughts or feelings you indicated above occur, tell yourself STOP.
- Repeat STOP until your mind is focused on that word.
- Then tell yourself to take a deep breath; mentally count to three.
- Slowly let it out while thinking RELAX.
- Take another deep breath; mentally count to three. Slowly let it out while thinking RELAX.
- Visualize the angry episode again.
- Repeat this process at least one more time.

Again from chapter 1:

Choose another current angry episode:

What thoughts and feelings occurred during this incident?

Using the same process as you did on the first episode, visualize the new incident. As soon as the thoughts or feelings you indicated above occur, tell yourself to STOP, command yourself to breathe and continue the relaxation process. Repeat this process at least one more time using the same episode.

In both episodes, each time you inhaled deeply and commanded yourself to relax, your internal, physiological reaction slowed down to counteract the adrenaline. In essence, you used your new brain to override the effects of your old brain and old beliefs registered in the new brain.

4. USE A NONTHREATENING APPROACH

Recently a colleague and I were killing some time waiting for eight adolescents to appear for group therapy. Both of us were leaning back in our chairs, legs stretched out, arms loose, when I asked, "What would you say are some basic, general guidelines when responding to another person's anger?" Immediately he answered, "Be nonthreatening." I said, "Well, of course. Could you be more specific? Give me details of how to be less threatening." He said something glib. We both chuckled.

Then he sat up, leaned forward, and rubbed his forehead. He said, "First, I think men and women need to be approached differently. A woman is less threatened when she can see what is coming at her. So, when a woman is angry and I go to respond to her, I walk up directly in front of her. With an angry man, on the other hand, I approach from the side. Coming directly, head-on, face-to-face, at a man can be interpreted as a challenge. I have broken up a lot of fights by walking up next to a guy and saying, 'Look, this guy is a jerk. So what! There are times you've been a real jerk. Leave him alone. Let's go.' I really believe that there were times when, if I had said it to the guy's face, he would have hit me. By going at him from the side, I wasn't a threat and he was able to listen."

This was the first and only time I have heard this theory about approaching males and females from different directions. I have never read any empirical studies to support or negate my colleague's theory. But I decided to put it in this chapter because it obviously works for him and so it might help someone else.

Whether you approach an angry person from the front or the side or remain seated in your chair, it is imperative that you remain nonthreatening. If you are physically tense, this will heighten the person's anxiety. Anxiety is a form of fear, and fear signals the body that there is a threat. This means that you must know how to relax your body quickly. You can learn to do this easily by using the relaxation technique from the previous section.

You need to make two minor adjustments while performing the technique: you are going to do it without anyone noticing, and you will be alert, with your eyes open.

- Repeat STOP until your mind is focused on that word.
- Tell yourself to take a deep breath (take this breath in a way that no one knows how long or deep it is); mentally count to three.
- Slowly let it out (still no one knows) while thinking RELAX.
- Take another deep breath (surreptitiously); mentally count to three.
- Slowly let it out while thinking RELAX.

Also, pay attention to your body. Make sure that your hands are not balled into fists, a very tense posture and threatening gesture. Pay attention to your jaw. Stressed, tense people have mandibular problems because they clench their teeth. The harder your teeth are clenched, the more rigid your face looks. Open your mouth slightly. This will relax your jaw. The softer and more relaxed your face appears, the less of a threat you are.

Learning to gain control of your physiological reaction by employing your mind and using your body as described above is essential. Not only does it reduce the likelihood that the angry person will escalate aggressively, it also assists you in lowering the probability that you will respond defensively. The skills involved in responding to another's anger, no matter what your goal is for the outcome, can only be implemented when you have the ability to accurately assess environmental cues and use that information to make conscious decisions about your behavior. To achieve this, you need to override the danger signals of the purely instinctive old brain by using conscious thought from your new brain.

Because the quick relaxation technique outlined above works and because you will be able to more easily access it if you see it a number of times, I will write out the relaxation technique almost every time it accompanies a skill or technique, even when only minor alterations are required. As tedious as it may seem, I recommend you read it entirely, employing the same speed or rhythm you use when performing the task.

The expectation of a behavioral outcome, a product of internalized social misinformation, often triggers a person's instinctive alarm that warns of danger. For example, chapter 2 talks about the erroneous idea that anger always equates to danger. The belief that anger results in very harmful activity results in high anxiety whenever angry feelings occur. This leads to body tension. Whatever your expectations of the behavioral outcome are, they can be negated, resulting in lowered anxiety.

Look back to chapter 2, and list one piece of misinformation that you have been led to believe.

What is the truth that counteracts this misinformation?

Using your tape recorder or the verbal relaxation session, become relaxed. When your mind is clear, keeping the same rhythm that helped you relax, consciously negate the misinformation and add the accurate information. For example, "Anger is not a weapon. Anger is a feeling." While still relaxed, repeat the negation and information sentences three to five times. Make this a part of your daily relaxation sessions. Choose a different incident each day until you are able to hear angry feelings without shutting down emotionally because of fear. You can choose a different piece of misinformation for each session, making sure that the accurate information counteracts it.

5. ASK FOR CLARIFICATION

Do not attempt to read minds, because you cannot read minds. This does not mean that you are in any way inadequate. It simply means there is too much room for error. People's behaviors are easily misinterpreted because our evaluations of those behaviors are usually tainted by information from our personal history, belief system, or fears.

People say: "He's angry because he thinks I lied to him." "She's angry because she's jealous." "She's angry at me because I betrayed her." "He acts angry because he's afraid of intimacy." When I hear such statements, I say, "Well, it is pretty clear that he [or she] is angry. Did he tell you it was because you lied to him?" Or "Did she say it's because she is jealous?" About 90 percent of the time, the response I get back is, "Well, no. He [or she] would never admit that." My next question, "Then how do you know?" is answered, "I just know."

The reality is that we do not know. We only think we know. Until the angry person says the words or communicates the nature of the displeasure in other ways, we are attempting to mind read. Because reading minds is so open to misinterpretation, any response we make concerning that person's anger has a high probability of being ineffective.

There is a simple remedy to this situation. Ask for clarification. "John, I know you're angry. Is it because you think I lied? Or is it because you are jealous? Or, is it because you think I betrayed you?"

This technique works only if two conditions are met. First, you must ask the question sincerely and nondefensively. Second, you must be willing to take no for an answer. If you must be right, do not ask the question. It will lead to an argument that feeds the destructive anger. Besides that, why ask a question when you believe you know the answer? That will seem condescending, and the other person's angry feelings will grow.

Many people tend to believe that if anger is brought into the open through discussion it will escalate. In chapter 7, when I talk about intimacy, I will discuss in depth the fallacy of this idea. For now, suffice it to say, asking for clarification in a nondefensive way will create less anger than either responding to a misinterpretation of the angry person's feeling motives or not responding at all.

In addition to asking for clarification on what might be triggering a person's anger, another important skill is the ability to ask for clarification on what the angry person actually said. Because we hear through the ears of our history, what we think we've heard may not be what was said.

An extreme example might be a young woman whose father, when angry, would rant about how she was a stupid idiot. She may have noticed that whenever her supervisor calls her in to his office, her stomach tightens and her thoughts become defensive. Her anxiety builds as she walks toward his domain. Running through her head is a list of possible mistakes that might be attributed to her. Finally, she is seated in front of him, with the door closed. In a firm voice, he makes just one statement, "Your report had a few errors." She blows. She is extremely defensive, blaming others or the work conditions. In the back of her mind, she thinks, "Who is he to be so critical? What does he know?"

Ironically, if I asked this woman, "What were the exact words that your supervisor said?" she would be able to tell me. And if she is like many people in similar situations, her face would register surprise. The incident invokes such a strong negative self-message that it drowns out the supervisor's actual words. The more vehemently she expresses her anger, the greater the strength of her internal messages.

Responding to Today's Reality

You can avoid misinterpreting situations in two ways. First, use the quick relaxation technique with self-talk you have practiced.

- As you feel your anxiety rising, mentally repeat the word *STOP* until your mind is focused.
- Take a deep breath; hold it to the count of three.
- Slowly let it out, thinking the word *RELAX*.
- Take another deep breath; hold it to the count of three.
- Slowly let it out, thinking the word *RELAX*.

The second way you could help yourself would be to ask yourself exactly what was said.

- As you sense your own anger and defensiveness rising, mentally repeat the word *STOP* until your thoughts are focused.
- Take a deep breath; hold it to the count of three.
- Slowly let it out, telling yourself, "I can relax; this is not my father. This is my supervisor."
- Take another deep breath; hold it to the count of three.
- Slowly let it out, telling yourself, "Relax, listen to his words."

When you are sure of the words spoken, respond to the content of the words only. You stopped reading minds earlier in this section. Therefore, do not try to read between the lines or add any meaning beyond what is contained in the words. If a facial expression or tone of voice seems to indicate an additional message, nondefensively ask for clarification. Then respond to the clarified message.

6. PRESENT AN ATTITUDE OF RESPECT

I have asked thousands of people what makes them angry. Almost all of them have included rudeness, inconsiderateness, and impoliteness. These words indicate disrespect. Within each culture, people expect to be treated in certain ways. People look for behaviors that indicate they are valued members of the community. If someone is treated in a manner contrary to those expected behaviors, the response is labeled rude, inconsiderate, and impolite—in other words, disrespectful. Because one of anger's functions is to set the parameters of socially acceptable behavior, responding to a person's anger with disrespect quickly increases the intensity of the angry feelings. A potential problem when discussing respectful behaviors is that different cultural groups have differing ideas of what actions (and nonactions) constitute rude, impolite, and inconsiderate behaviors.

If you really do not know why someone is mad or you suspect the anger was triggered by an action on your part, take a deep breath to calm yourself and remember the importance of clarifying your interpretations. Begin by asking if you have offended the person in some way. At this point, you need to hope that the person has enough respect for you to be honest. When someone indicates that you have given offense and, upon hearing this, you feel some remorse, then let the other person know that you did not mean to offend, apologize sincerely, and if necessary ask what other behaviors you can use in the future. If you are told you've stepped on another person's social toes and you do not feel remorse, then do not apologize. Simply say that you did not mean to offend and that you will attempt to avoid doing it again.

A general attitude of respect will serve you well when a hostile person's anger erupts aggressively. One afternoon, I was working on a hospital chemical dependency unit when I heard a great commotion from a patient's room. Mr. Jenkins, the patient, had his suitcase on the bed. He was throwing his clothes into it and muttering. When he ran out of clothes to throw, he started throwing furniture. I went to the door and looked in. I looked around and saw his counselor was right behind me. So I asked, "Mr. Jenkins, will you speak with your counselor about what is bothering you?" He replied, "No. I get no respect. They have shown me no respect. I don't want to talk with anyone. I want to leave." I asked, "Mr. Jenkins, have I ever treated you with disrespect?"

He stopped ranting and throwing things, thought for a moment, and, when he answered no, I asked, "Then will you talk with me?" When he agreed, I went in, sat down, and we talked. He did finish packing and left the unit. But at least he stopped breaking our furniture.

Some of you may be wondering, what if he had said yes, that I had treated him with disrespect? The answer to that question is in the next section.

7. YOU DO NOT ALWAYS HAVE TO BE RIGHT

Let go of the need to be right or to always have the answer. If Mr. Jenkins had answered that I had shown disrespect toward him, I would have responded, "Please, tell me when and how I did that. I do not want to offend you again."

In a country such as the United States, where dissimilar cultures rub up against each other, there are times when we offend one another, when we make social mistakes, when we are in the wrong. Sweeping these gaffes under the proverbial carpet that hides all errors and then pretending that the lump in that carpet is someone else's dirty wrongdoing requires us to erect defenses to hide our guilt. Defensive responses to another person's anger, whether defenses of avoidance or of blame, lead to the escalating sequence of events described in chapter 4.

People who project an appearance of always having to be right usually have a negative self-message of "I am wrong." Remember, this self-message is not "I do some things wrong." It is "As a human being, I am somehow terribly, deeply, defectively wrong." And it is a lie. This particular false assessment encourages that person to interpret other people's anger as an accusation, obligating the individual to defend his or her sense of adequacy.

People with a strong need to be right want to "do it right," to know just the right answer to another person's angry outburst. Any answer that is presented humanely and with respect is just the right answer. Some techniques provide a higher probability of success, but if you are anxious about applying them with absolute correctness, you will not be effective.

A Quick Affirmation

If you think you may have some of the tendencies described above, here is an exercise that may help you. In the evening, during your relaxation session, when you become relaxed and your mind is clear, repeat three times "I am a worthwhile person who is allowed to make mistakes." Continue to do this exercise with each relaxation session until the sentence, or a part of it, automatically pops into your thoughts during routine activities.

8. REVIEW YOUR LANGUAGE

Some words and phrases tend to provoke defensiveness even though their literal meaning has no provocative content. To respond effectively to another person's ire, it is important that you identify these words and phrases and limit their use. Otherwise, you may find yourself performing the response techniques properly, use one of these words, and inadvertently escalate the destructive anger.

But

But is a word that can drive people crazy. It drives me crazy. I hear it and I know that the person is going to negate what he just said. "I want to stop using marijuana, but I keep going to bong parties." "I like your new hairdo, but . . ." At the *but*, I know the person dislikes my new haircut. *But* often gives conflicting messages and puts the listener on the defensive. To me, "Yes, but . . ." means "no" and "I agree with you, but . . ." translates to "I disagree with you." If you can replace the word *but* with the word *and* so that the sentence still makes sense, then you have a sentence that is presenting congruent messages. For example, the sentence "I want to stop using marijuana, but I don't know how" can be used, excluding the *but*, without the first part of the sentence being contradicted. If it does not make sense, then you have two competing ideas. In this situation it is most helpful to decide which idea is most accurate, present it, and forgo the other thought until later.

You

When using the pronoun *you*, take care to avoid verbally trapping the person or giving the impression that you are being incriminatory. Statements that begin with "You make me feel . . ." "If you hadn't . . ." "You are . . ." or "You feel . . ." sound accusatory and maneuver the person into a psychological corner. A natural reaction is to come out of that corner ready for a fight.

I Know How You Feel

The two closely related sentences "I know how you feel," and "I feel your pain," are almost certain to escalate already heightened anger arousal. First, these statements are not true. Until science makes it possible for one human being to enter the skin of another and experience the same internal reaction, an understanding of how another person feels is tenuous at best. We can imagine how we might feel if we were in the same situation. If we have gone through a similar incident, we can experience empathy and compassion. That is all we are capable of experiencing of another's feelings, including pain. Individuals experience their own pain. Second, to someone who's angry, these statements sound condescending, as though they lessen the importance of the feelings involved.

Once I was doing some consulting work for a department of social services in a relatively large city. I was walking through the main hallway to a conference room when I heard a chair crash. I went to the office where the sound had originated and looked in. I saw a large woman, holding an infant close to her with one arm and grasping the hand of a toddler with her other hand, standing over the desk of the case worker. I will never forget the words she vehemently spat at that worker: "You know how I feel? You know how I feel? When you have thirteen kids to feed and no money, then you know how I feel."

Later that day I went back and talked with the worker. She had been to a communication workshop the month before where she was taught to show empathy by using the phrase "I know how you feel." Empathy is good when you want to reduce anger. Unfortunately, that phrase does not present a very convincing empathetic demeanor. I asked the worker how she would feel if she were in the woman's situation. She said, "I would be very scared." I then suggested that she express her empathy using specifics: "Be honest. Let her know that if you were in her place, you would feel scared." That sounds so much more truthful and so much more real. It also shows that you are not glibly throwing out phrases to try to calm the person down. You had to stop and imagine the situation long enough to come up with a specific feeling.

Why

The word *why*, such a short utterance, can provoke a large amount of trouble. Originally intended to elicit information to provide clarification, *why* is so misused as a means of expressing anger and allocating blame that its utterance, even when appropriate, has the power to precipitate a cluster of negative reactions.

Think of the "why" questions you were asked as a child: "Why did you hit your sister?" "Why is your room such a mess?" "Why are you always getting into trouble?" "Why can't you do anything right?" "Why can't you be more like your brother?" These questions are not asking for information. In fact, there are no logical answers that would satisfy the asker. Underneath these questions is a great deal of destructive anger, accusations, and put-downs. Young people exposed to this type of question over time learn to connect the word *why* to the hurtful sensations that it attempts to mask. When this happens, they interpret *why* as a warning signal that potential pain is nearby and get ready to defend themselves.

To obtain information, especially from someone who is angry, avoid "why" questions by asking, "Can you tell me what was going on when . . . ?" or "Would you describe what happened?"

A closely related question is "What were you thinking?" These four words are usually strung together on a tone of voice that expands the phrase to "What were you thinking, you idiot?" For all the same reasons that I recommend you avoid *why*, I also recommend you avoid this phrase. Instead, if you do need to know what the person was thinking at the time an incident occurred, questions such as "What thoughts did you have when . . . ?" or "Can you tell me what your strongest thought was before you . . . ?" are more likely to provide the information you are seeking while producing less defensiveness.

Should and Its Relations

The words *should, ought, must,* and *you have to* tend to trigger hostility. The words *ought* and *should* have two basic objectives. The first is to deposit one person's values onto another person. In so doing, these words can be emotionally threatening. For example, "You ought to go on to college"

and "You should honor your parents" may sound harmless. The problem
can be easily understood, however, when I put them in context. The first
sentence was said to a boy who could barely read, hated studying, and had
a proclivity for fixing cars. In his mind he needed to pursue his vocation.
The second statement was directed at a young woman whose father sexually molested her weekly from age six to thirteen.

The second reason that *should* (or *ought to*) elicits a negative reaction is
that people often use it to evaluate someone else's behavior as indicating poor
judgment. "You should have gone straight home from school and you would
not have been attacked." "You should not have invested all your money in
one stock." "You should have known better." These statements are accusatory, judgmental, and of little value because the actions that they are evaluating have already happened. They are in the past. They cannot be changed.

You must and *you have to* tend to stimulate defensive reactions because
they demand someone behave in a certain way. If that person has any spark
of defiance, it will be ignited into a flame when the words *you must* or *you
have to* are directed at him or her. Workers in a variety of jobs have told me
that their clients have to do certain things or there are consequences. So the
clients have to comply. Well, no, they do not. They can choose to incur the
consequences.

I work in a treatment program that offers services to adolescents, a
number of whom will be remanded to a juvenile detention system, eu-
phemistically called training school, if they do not complete our program.
My colleagues and I regularly remind some of those adolescents of the
choice they can make. We outline what needs to be accomplished to complete our program and avoid training school. Then we outline the behaviors
that are inhibiting their ability to complete our program, taking them toward training school. We explain that it may not be much of a choice, yet it
is theirs and we will assist them with whichever direction they choose. This
is not done with sarcasm. It is done with deep respect for their right to decide how they want to live their lives.

Reducing Anger-Provoking Language

Of the words and phrases below, which ones do you use often? You can add
words to the list. What can you say instead?

Word/Phrase	Replacement Word/Phrase
But	
You	
I know how you feel	
Why	
What were you thinking	
Should *or* ought	

Who is available to point out when you use the words and phrases you marked above?

at home: _____

at work: _____

at other places/functions: _____

Ask the people you listed above to help you. Explain that you would appreciate it if they would quietly indicate when they hear you using the words that you want to replace. Once they point the word or phrase out, respond by saying the new word or phrase that you want to put in its place.

List any circumstances in which you tend to say, "you must" or "you have to." What are the consequences of the choices that you can present to that person instead?

Circumstance:

Choices	Consequences

Circumstance:

<u>Choices</u>   <u>Consequences</u>

Circumstance:

<u>Choices</u>   <u>Consequences</u>

9. POSITIVELY RELIVE THE INCIDENT

After an angry episode, people have a propensity to relive the incident mentally using either a depressive or aggressive response style. People who externalize replay the incident by changing their part of the script to indicate what they could have said, should have said, or will say next time. Usually the new lines are sarcastic, hurtful, or blaming. People who internalize during their replay tend to berate themselves with questions such as "Why didn't I stand up for myself?" or "Why was I so nasty?" Neither of these activities produce positive results. The first prepares people to be outwardly aggressive and keeps the adrenaline increased long after the threat and danger is gone. The second type of reliving directs people's negative thoughts and energy at themselves, which lowers their self-esteem and results in greater anxiety during future anger episodes.

Productive Mental Reenactments

A more productive reliving can be done when you find a skill described in this book that you particularly like and would like to try. Choose a skill and then, with the relaxation technique you have been using, relax and help your mind become clear. When your mind is clear:

- Imagine the scene and what the angry person is saying.
- Remaining calm, visualize yourself responding to the angry person using the new behavior.
- If the new behavior does not seem comfortable, change it just a little and try again.
- Continue doing this until it is easy to see yourself performing the new technique.

10. KEEP IN MIND RELAXATION, COMMUNICATION, AND RESPECT

This chapter presents a host of ideas, suggestions, and new behaviors. It may seem too much to remember or take in at once, but if you look carefully, you will notice that there are only three basic themes that wind their way through the sections in this chapter. They are relaxation, communication, and respect.

Relaxation is necessary to reduce anxiety. This allows you to be less defensive and less of a threat to the angry person. Also, relaxation sessions prepare your mind to incorporate new behaviors more easily and learn new ways of thinking. Practicing new behaviors in your mind before trying them in actuality makes them easier to implement. I used to play on a softball team every summer. One summer I increased my batting average by a hundred points. The only thing I did differently from the year before was to use relaxation/visualization techniques.

I am convinced that 75 percent of all angry altercations are the result of poor communication. You cannot respond well if you have misinterpreted what was said and do not know the effect your words have on others. Therefore, listen carefully, clarify often, and develop an awareness of the impact your language has on other people.

Respect for yourself translates into keeping yourself safe and acting in ways that benefit you without extracting a price from others. It is difficult to like yourself when in the process of hurting or denigrating someone else. Demonstrating respectful behaviors toward other people elevates personal self-esteem while reducing perceived threats. Both outcomes can reduce hostile defensiveness.

This chapter presented a variety of methods for using relaxation, communication, and respect when confronted with anger. They are not necessarily the only ways. If you have other means to keep these themes in mind, use them, or adapt them to the methods described here. Successful use of the techniques outlined in the remainder of the book do not depend on how you attain and maintain these three themes, only that you use them as the foundation upon which you build your skills.

6

Defusion Techniques

PERHAPS YOU ARE A TEACHER, waiting to keep an appointment with an irate parent whose child has just been suspended. Maybe you work in the human service field as a child and protective service worker or a mental health worker, conducting interviews to collect sensitive information. You may serve through your local government as a driver's license examiner, police officer, or building inspector. Chances are, no matter what your vocation, you occasionally encounter belligerence from those you serve. Then again, you could be similar to some people I have met who quickly inform me they have no problems with clients or customers—they expect customers to be argumentative. The people they find intolerable are contentious and explosive co-workers, especially supervisors.

The majority of American adults spend approximately two thousand hours a year at the workplace. If you dread the irate consumers of your product or services or if you spend too much time attempting to avoid the incendiary vituperations of middle management, then that two thousand hours a year begins to look like an eternity of torture. It becomes depressing and upsetting, and the people you come home to experience the fallout from your stressful day. Believe it or not, working under these conditions is often unnecessary.

Here are six specific methods, what I call *defusion techniques,* that can be quite effective in deflating hostility: listening for and responding to the fear, listening for and responding to the self-message, providing a new interpretation, being of good humor, doing the unexpected, and using emotional honesty. I use them most often at work because that is where I encounter the greatest number of aggressive episodes. But I have found these techniques to be useful in social and domestic situations as well.

Each technique addresses a certain component of the feeling circle. They can be used separately or in combination. I urge you to try each one. Adapt the ones you find most comfortable to fit your own personality. This is important. Otherwise these techniques will appear to be manipulative gimmicks, resulting in the other person's anger increasing rather than defusing. When adapting one of the techniques, be sure that you address the other person in a respectful manner.

Before you try any of these defusion techniques, it is essential for you to make sure that you are responding from the perspective of an adult rather than the experiences of a child. In addition, all of the techniques require accurate listening skills. Here's an exercise that will help you negate old expected behaviors and at the same time help you self-command your mind to listen.

As we discussed in chapter 1, we developed our expectations of others' angry behaviors during early childhood years. Those expectations are not real to the current situation, however, because you are no longer a child facing a large, powerful adult who has the authority to hurt you physically. Therefore, understanding your specific expectations of the outcome when someone is angry (do you expect to be hit, demeaned, ignored, etc.?), actively asserting that this expectation is not real (this person is not the caregiver who punished, this client is not the father with power, etc.), and replacing the unreal expectation with a reality-based statement (he can't punish me, he doesn't have the power), will help you listen more clearly to an angry person's communication.

Look back at the exercises in chapter 1 (pages 10–11).

When your caregiver was angry with you, how was that anger expressed?

What did you learn to expect from angry people?

How is this expectation no longer based in reality?

What short statement of reality would negate the unreal expectation?

Did you have another caregiver that influenced your expectation of how expressed anger might be dangerous or hurtful?

What did you learn to expect from this?

What short statement of reality would negate this unreal expectation?

During your relaxation time, the following visualization and affirmation will help you replace the nonreality-based expectation with the reality statement and will focus your attention on listening. Use your relaxation tape or exercise to become physically loose and mentally clear. Then visualize an angry episode that involved a customer (someone who buys services or goods). Start the visualization from the beginning of the incident. As the customer starts to become hostile:

- Tell yourself STOP until your thoughts subside.
- Take a deep breath and mentally count to three.
- As you slowly let it out, consciously tell yourself the true statement.
- Then command yourself to listen.

For example, if you were punished when your caregiver felt anger toward you, the exercise would go:

- STOP, STOP, STOP.
- Take a deep breath—one, two, three.
- Slowly let it out. This person can't punish me; he doesn't have the power.
- I'll listen and try to hear what he is saying.

Practice this exercise as you go through your day, even when no one is angry. There are many messages you can listen for. Later sections will suggest listening for the fear that resides under the anger or listening for the negative self-message that the anger protects. For this particular exercise, I recommend that you listen closely for any common goals you may have with the customer. Often these goals can be used to help an angry customer stay focused, while defusing the hostility.

I was challenged by a food stamp worker to meet her clients and to do her job for a day. I accepted the challenge provided she would get the approval of her supervisor and help me fill out the paperwork properly. Both conditions were met, and on a hot Monday morning in July, in a building with broken air conditioning, in the capital city of a southern state, I faced my first food stamp client. The day got hotter and more humid. The people got hotter and more irritable as they had to wait longer and longer.

It was deep into the afternoon when a woman came into my cubbyhole of an office, sat down, and immediately began complaining about the wait. After a long diatribe concerning her children's care, she said, "I have two girls coming home from school at three o'clock, and I have to be there." This sentence has a goal that both of us could benefit from. When she stopped for a breath, I said, "I can understand why a mother would want to be home for her kids after school." I looked at my watch and added, "It's about ten to two. If you will help me answer these questions, I think we can make it."

My response to her hostility accomplished three objectives: I validated her concerns about being home for her girls. I solicited her help. And while doing so, I made it clear that she had the responsibility in determining how long the interview would take. Establishing a mutual goal reduced the material she had to argue about and turned her attention to a common task, allowing us to work together instead of engaging in a tug-of-war.

As the interview went on, we came to a place where the questionnaire asked for the father for each of her five children. With the first child, she began to hesitate, answering with, "I don't know. What does it matter? I can't remember his name. I met him at a party." When she continued this same routine of resistance with the second child on the list, I calmly put my pencil down, took a deep breath, and in a gentle voice said, "Mrs. Johnson, if we keep going like this, we are never going to get out of here before three o'clock." For a moment she was speechless. Then she rattled off the remaining four names for me. Were they real? I have no idea. My job that day was to get the information, not to verify it.

Active, focused listening will provide you with numerous clues on how to respond in specific situations. Hearing what people are attempting to communicate, as well as their actual words, to the exclusion of your own internal reactions and conditioned expectations is a skill that will be helpful as you try the first defusion technique.

LISTENING FOR AND RESPONDING TO THE FEAR

This defusion technique is directed at the Emotion component of the feeling circle. It takes into account the fact that anger is never a primary emotional reaction. The internal physiological sensation that signals the presence of anger occurs after, or secondary to, a fear reaction. Anger acts as a defense mechanism to hide fear. Either bringing the fear to the open in a nonthreatening manner or assuaging the fear extinguishes the need for a defensive posture. No matter what your profession is, the people seeking your product or service may enter your place of business with fear just below the surface. Imagine, if they were to speak honestly, how their fears would sound.

- At a car dealership: I am afraid of being cheated.
- At a hospital: I am afraid of dying. I am afraid of losing control.
- At the department of social services: I need help and I am afraid you won't help me.
- At a real estate agency: I am afraid I am making a terrible mistake and the payments will be too much for me to handle.
- In a classroom: I am afraid you will laugh at me.

Paying attention to the fear below the anger is easier on the listener's emotions than withstanding a barrage of angry words. If you do not believe me, imagine your last angry customer. Remember exactly what she said, her tone of voice, and how you felt listening. Now, think of a fear that she may have about being in your place of business. Imagine her telling you the fear. How has your emotional state changed?

Once you have identified the fear, you can respond to it in one of two ways, addressing it directly or indirectly. Approaching the person's fear directly is the best course when you are sure that the person will not feel ashamed for being afraid. If there is shame, the person usually creates more hostility in an attempt to hide the fear.

I witnessed an ultrasound technician deftly employ this technique last week when I went for my annual mammogram. Actually, it was my second visit, as I was called and asked to come back that day for another type of mammogram that would help them look at a specific area of concern. I went. I was nervous. I attempted to cover it by being irritable. I had the second test, becoming more nervous and more irritable. After the second test, the technician came in, told me that the second test had not cleared up the problem and they wanted to do an ultrasound.

Now I started to panic. They shuffled me over to another area of the building. I was asked to sit. I waited for fifteen minutes. Finally, the ultrasound technician arrived, took me into the room, and left me alone again. By now my imagination was going wild, and I was ready to fight. I decided I would not do anything more until I found out what was going on. The woman came hurrying in again and told me to lie down on the table as she moved to the machine. I remained standing, my arms crossed. The thought "I will be damned if I am getting on any table without some explanation first" focused my angry energy.

She looked up, saw me still standing there, and her face changed. It was as though she suddenly remembered something very important. She walked to where I was standing and said, "A lot of women tell me they are scared when they get sent here. They think something must be wrong or the doctor wouldn't have ordered another test."

My anger washed away immediately. She was so skillful in this technique that she not only brought my fear out into the open, she let me know it is normal (a lot of women told her) to be feeling frightened in this situation. Another skill she exhibited was her ability to present the idea of my being afraid without trapping me. She never said, "You are scared." Speaking about other women, she left me a way out. I could have responded with a variety of denials, including, "Well, I am not feeling that way." Since she was quite accurate with her assessment, I told her so and we went on with the test.

Toward the end of the ultrasound, she explained that because she was not a doctor, she was not permitted to tell me anything that she saw or did not see on the ultrasound. Then she added, "You know what I can say? If it were me on that table, I would relax and not worry."

Afraid or *scared* may be too strongly descriptive for some people. Words such as *anxious, nervous,* or *worried* can be used in their stead as less threatening descriptions of fear. Once someone has brought the fear out into the open, there is no longer any need for the anger to continue hiding it. It is like the child's game of hide-and-seek. Once you are found, you may as well give up and come out. Of course there are exceptions.

There are people whom you do not want to approach with the idea that they could be feeling fear. This type of person honestly believes that he (it usually is a he, although I have met some women with this mind-set) never feels afraid. If you were to suggest that he does have this "unmanly" sensation, he would intensify the anger to prove you wrong.

Whether he feels the underlying emotion or not, where there is anger, it is generated by fear. Reducing the fear or putting it to rest alleviates the hostility, especially in this personality type. This can be accomplished in an indirect way that does not threaten this person's machismo. The three-step process for doing this is:

- Listen for what the person fears.
- Figure out a personality trait that the individual has that would overcome the fear.
- Let the individual know that he has that trait.

I was working in private practice when, about one o'clock in the afternoon my intercom went off. There was a walk-in client waiting to be seen. This particular client, a man named Steve, had been sent over from a doctor who, suspecting alcoholism, wanted an assessment and, if necessary, for Steve to be sent to the nearest hospital for detoxification. I opened my door to the waiting room and greeted Steve and his wife. I introduced myself and invited them into my office. Steve no sooner got into my office and sat down than he started saying, "I ain't going to no damned detox place. They have bars on the windows. They tie you down."

I did not know this man and, other than getting sober, I was not sure what he feared. With some hostile people, you do not need to know what the exact fear might be. I did notice, however, that he came out fighting.

I thought, "He's a fighter. He's got courage." When he stopped to take a breath, I said, "You're right, it takes courage to stop drinking."

He acted like he did not hear me. He kept going with his tirade. "They make you drink that nasty stuff. They don't know what they are doing. Damn doctors stick you with needles."

He took a breath and I said, "I agree, it takes a lot of courage to go to detox." He and I did this verbal dance for a couple more rounds. With each go around, his voice lost some of its belligerence and became softer. When I knew that he could hear my words, I said, "And Steve, I think you have the courage." Steve stopped talking and looked at me. So I added, "Let's do an assessment and see if you need to use that courage." It turned out that Steve was late-stage alcohol dependent. His wife signed him in to the detox center by three that afternoon.

You may have noticed two glaring characteristics about the interchange between Steve and me. In order for him to hear the positive trait that I thought he possessed, I had to repeat the concept a number of times. Part of this may have been due to the fact that Steve had been drinking. A large part had to do with his mind focusing hard to manufacture reasons to be angry in order to defend against feeling the fear.

The second characteristic of our dialogue, which is typical of the indirect approach, is that it sounded like two separate conversations. Steve's monologue expounded on his misconceived notions of detoxification centers, while mine focused on courage. As crazy and disparate as the two conversations may sound, when implementing the indirect approach to assuaging the angry person's fear, it is important not to get sidetracked and pulled into the angry argument. The whole point of the argument is to keep you away from discovering the angry person's fright. If I had gotten hooked into arguing whether or not there are bars on the windows, I would have been drawn into Steve's way of avoiding the fear that lives just under his anger's surface.

Identifying and Responding to the Underlying Fear

The questions and exercises below will help you be more comfortable implementing the above technique. The first exercise has to do with identifying and addressing the underlying fear in hypothetical situations. Think about someone you know well, who would not be threatened by having personal fears addressed. Then imagine that person entering the businesses listed earlier. What do you think the fear would be? How could you use the direct approach to bring the fear out in a way that does not emotionally trap the individual? In thinking about the indirect approach, what personal characteristic does the person have that could overcome the fear? How could you remind the person that he or she has this characteristic?

Car Dealership:
The fear is

A direct statement concerning the fear is

The characteristic that the person has to overcome the fear is

An indirect statement reminding the person of this characteristic is

Hospital:
The fear is

A direct statement concerning the fear is

The characteristic that the person has to overcome the fear is

An indirect statement reminding the person of this characteristic is

Department of Social Services:
The fear is

A direct statement concerning the fear is

The characteristic that the person has to overcome the fear is

An indirect statement reminding the person of this characteristic is

Real Estate Agency:
The fear is

A direct statement concerning the fear is

The characteristic that the person has to overcome the fear is

An indirect statement reminding the person of this characteristic is

Classroom:
The fear is

A direct statement concerning the fear is

The characteristic that the person has to overcome the fear is

An indirect statement reminding the person of this characteristic is

   Think of your place of employment and the people you sell to, provide a service for, or negotiate with, then list some fears that you think your customers might experience. How could you respond to each fear in a direct way and an indirect way? Remember to keep your responses short. You will attempt to employ them during a time of stress. The shorter they are, the easier they are to remember. Also, the more succinct, the more likely they are to be cognitively processed by the receiver.

1. Customer's probable fear:

A direct response is

An indirect response is

2. Customer's probable fear:

A direct response is

An indirect response is

3. Customer's probable fear:

A direct response is

An indirect response is

One way to ensure that the responses you have decided on are at the ready during an angry encounter is to mentally practice them during your relaxation session. Do your relaxation exercise for ten minutes. When your mind is free and clear, using the same rhythm you used to become relaxed, repeat three times the response you have chosen to implement.

Think of a specific angry customer you have dealt with in your place of business. What are some specific statements that this person has made? What fears are those statements protecting? Decide whether the direct approach or the indirect approach would more effectively address this customer's fear. Write out the exact words that you can use to implement your response.

Angry customer's statements:

What fear(s) are being protected:

Response to the fear:

    To further imprint the response on your brain, visualize a customer. Remember a time when she was angry and what she was saying. In the visualization, respond in the new way. If the response does not seem comfortable to you, change it a little and try again. Do this until it suits you and you can say the words easily.

    Throughout this section I have presented ideas specific to the workplace. The responses have been aimed at individuals on the other side of the desk: the customers, patients, students, guests, taxpayers, clients, passengers, and on and on and on. This response technique, as with any of the following techniques, is also effective with your supervisor, co-workers, bridge partners, teammates, and department store clerks, even your adolescent child.

    In the exercise above, replace your customer with one of these other people. Ask and answer the same questions and then do the same type of visualization. Please use discernment. It is one thing to say to your seventeen-year-old daughter, "It sounds to me like you are afraid to fail," and quite another to point out your supervisor's fear of failure. In most cases, prudence dictates an indirect approach when responding to colleagues.

LISTENING FOR AND RESPONDING TO THE SELF-MESSAGE

This particular technique directs the Reaction component, the point where the responder enters the angry person's feeling circle, toward the Thought component. The first skill the responder needs is the ability to listen for and identify the angry person's self-evaluation. When the situation is not physically dangerous, the person who behaves aggressively is protecting a negative self-message. The protected message could be one of an infinite number of possibilities: I'm degraded by being here, I'm not important, I'm wrong, I'm a failure, I'm no good, I'm worthless.

I have two hints on how to listen for the underlying self-message. First, the negative self-statement will be clearest and strongest in the first two or three sentences spoken by the angry person. In fact, that person may use the exact words involved in the self-message. Second, the verbalized message will be the opposite of the negative self-message. For me to explain this phenomenon, I need you to look at figure C on page 56 or figure D on page 67, both in chapter 4. Locate the dotted line that crosses the figure in the Emotion area between Fear/Anxiety and Anger. Notice that everything above the line could be described using words such as *vulnerable, open to attack, powerless,* while everything below the line indicates *strength, ready to fight, powerful.* They are opposites. Some may argue that suicide does not look like a very strong behavior. But its strength has been used as a device to manipulate others. In fact, its impact on the living can continue long after the person's death.

Since the angry person's words are the opposite of his or her self-evaluation, the statement a friend of mine made during a stressful situation, "Don't they know I'm too important to trifle with!" indicated the underlying self-evaluation: "I'm not important." Someone who always has to prove a point and be right has a negative self-message that says, "I am wrong."

Sometimes the underlying self-message does not have to do with self-esteem. Instead, it can involve self-evaluation in a given situation. For example, a person sitting across from an IRS auditor or a loan officer or a state trooper with her ticket pad in hand may experience a strong sense of powerlessness over the situation. This might translate to "I am incapable of affecting this situation." If this person holds on to only the first three words, "I am incapable," another self-message with a similar meaning may be triggered.

The second skill involved in this defusion technique is to respond effectively to the identified self-statement. And as with the first defusion technique that required a response to the person's fear, this technique also requires choosing between a direct and an indirect response. I made a direct response to my friend who was ranting that he was too important to be trifled with. I chose the direct approach because we were friends, and I knew he trusted me. I said, "John, whether people trifle with you or not is no measure of how important you are."

The indirect approach is done a little differently when responding to a negative self-message than it is when addressing a person's fear. In this technique, all you have to do is refute the underlying statement. The loan officer talking with a woman who has a self-message of "I'm not capable" might say, "Ms. Parker, you may think that you do not have choices in this situation. You do. Here are some options open to you." Ms. Parker's fear and anger may block out the words of the loan officer. In that case, the bank officer can repeat, "You do have other choices" or "There are some other things you can do."

Many of the parents of the adolescents I work with come to the first counseling session thinking I am going to blame their child's chemical dependency on them. Or that I am going to inform them that if they had been better parents, their child would not be in my treatment center. They expect me to think this way because they are thinking this way. During the months or years that their child has been exhibiting symptoms of chemical dependency, they have been blaming themselves, and so they are defensively prepared for my condemnation. I have seen it time and again over the years. So, very shortly into the first session, I explain my philosophy of chemical dependency, making it very clear that I do not believe that they caused it. I also let them know that, as far as I can tell, they seem to be good parents. Normally at this point, they look puzzled. I go on to explain, "If you were bad parents, you would not be here today trying to help your son."

Some agencies inadvertently feed into their clientele's negative self-messages. If a man believes "I'm not important," and he arrives at an agency where he is given a number and told to wait in a waiting area that is overcrowded, noisy, and smelly, the probability is high that his negative self-evaluation has been confirmed and his anger is ready to explode by the time you meet with him.

You may not have the authority to rearrange your company's system in order to change this situation. But you can address the negative self-message in a way that alleviates some of the harm done by the system, and it will not cost you any extra time. When you go out to get the client, patient, or customer and you call his number, as soon as the person comes to you, ask his name and introduce yourself. As you show him back to your office, address that negative self-message by saying something to the effect of: "I know you had to wait awhile. I don't want you to think that it is because you are not important. Come in, sit down, and for the next thirty minutes, we'll focus on assisting you."

Applying a variation of this scenario is possible in a number of settings, including social service offices, clinics, and airports.

Recognizing Systemic Validation of Self-Messages

From your experiences, what negative self-messages do you think might be going on in your clientele? If you are in a human service profession, is there any social stigma attached to the people who receive your services? That stigma becomes a negative self-evaluation.

List three negative self-messages that might be triggered in your customers because of the stigma society may have placed on the people your workplace serves. How could you respond to that message directly and indirectly by refuting it?

1. Possible negative self-message:

Direct response:

Indirect response:

2. Possible negative self-message:

Direct response:

Indirect response:

3. Possible negative self-message:

Direct response:

Indirect response:

Which of the above responses would you be willing to say to your customers?

Are there any environmental conditions or systemic procedures in your place of business that might trigger your customers' negative self-messages? What actions or responses can you provide that would reduce the effects of those conditions or procedures?

Condition or procedure that could trigger negative messages:

The negative self-message triggered:

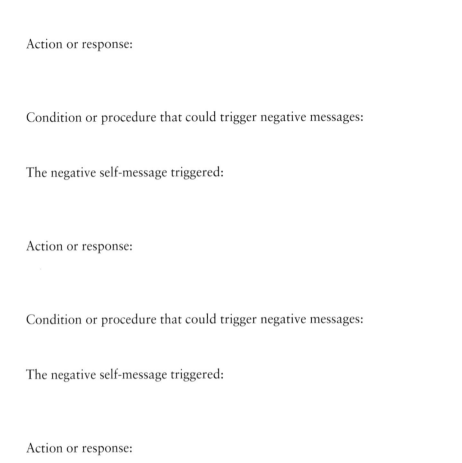

Action or response:

Condition or procedure that could trigger negative messages:

The negative self-message triggered:

Action or response:

Condition or procedure that could trigger negative messages:

The negative self-message triggered:

Action or response:

As you do your relaxation session, when your mind is clear and focused, repeat the responses you are comfortable saying at work until they seem natural to you. In your mind, replay the actions and responses that negate the effects that the environment or procedures have on your customers.

Responding to Specific Negative Self-Statements

People who use aggression to protect their negative self-messages are holding on to their dignity as best they can. Whether dealing with angry customers, friends, loved ones, or co-workers, you can assist their endeavors to protect their self-esteem and, in so doing, lower their aggression, by listening carefully for clues to each individual's self-message and by responding to that communication.

Remember the last aggressive tirade in which you were the target. What were some of the specific statements said by the aggressor?

Write out one possible negative self-evaluation triggering those statements:

How could you have responded directly to the triggering self-evaluation?

How could you have responded indirectly to the triggering self-evaluation?

During your relaxation session, envision the above episode. Remember the harsh words. Then:

- Command yourself to STOP.
- Take a deep breath and count to three.
- As you let it out slowly, tell yourself to listen to the underlying message.
- See yourself responding to that message.

Would you change any of your words? If so, go ahead. Then do the exercise again using the new words. Try doing this entire process again with another incident of aggression. The more often you use this process to practice, the easier it will be when another actual aggressive incident occurs to respond to the negative self-message.

Negative self-messages and unrealistic fears distort people's interpretations of events, making them seem more dangerous than they really are. If you can become adept at responding to people's fears and negative self-messages as described in these first two techniques, most of the hostility around you will dissipate. You may not feel comfortable using these techniques, or there may be times when you just cannot seem to get a handle on what fear is occurring or what the negative self-message is. In those instances, the following methods of responding can be helpful.

PROVIDING A NEW INTERPRETATION

Human beings interpret their surrounding world by sifting its events through their historical screens. People who are overly defensive have histories filled with punishment, ridicule, or victimization. This is what they have received from the past and what they expect from the future. Their hurtful life experiences and resultant expectations filter their interpretations of current events. They tend to see themselves as the center of all immediate incidents, forcing them to view events very personally. As a result, they see many of the events in their lives that do not go their way as something that has been done to them: "This is being done specifically to hurt me." "You are out to get me."

Many people instinctively know that this is going on with the hostile, defensive individual, and they attempt to shift the person's perspective. I have witnessed a bank teller, airline counter worker, mental health clinician, and an insurance receptionist, as well as three social services workers, trying to implement this technique by saying, "It is our policy." By blaming it on company policy, they are saying: "This is not about *you*. Don't take it personally. It's about decisions that the company has initiated without ever having met you." The workers are also attempting to direct the focus of the person's ire away from them and onto the company: "This is not my fault, it's the company's fault." Although the instincts in using this kind of technique were on the mark, none of these workers were very successful. They didn't apply the technique effectively.

To those who do not work for the company, the declaration "It's policy" has very little meaning. First, it is an abstract concept. Angry people are more likely to be thinking about their particular problem in concrete terms, and so they do not process the sentence. Second, the company policy has no meaning for customers. They have not held it, seen it, or studied it. To them, the policy does not exist. Since the policy is not real to them, they do not care what it says.

If you have used the "It's policy" method in the past and are tempted to use it again, I recommend you shift your approach just a little to make it more effective. You already know which policies cause the most problems. Make copies of the written policy and keep those copies nearby. The next time you are facing an angry customer and you have the urge to utter the words *It's policy,* stop yourself. Instead say, "Hold on. I want to show you something." Get your copy of the policy and lay it down on your work area to one side of you. Do not lay it directly in front of you. Then very deliberately take your hand and point to the area of the policy you want the person to read. The customer's head, eyes, and anger will go with your hand to the now-concrete policy. You may want to read that piece of policy out loud in case the customer cannot read.

This technique, focused on changing an angry person's interpretation, can be used in other situations. An example of how I used this technique to shift the perception of an entire room full of people occurred when I was an addiction counselor in a residential center. This was in the early 1980s, in a freestanding facility that had fifty patients. Two counselors were required to work each Saturday. We rotated Saturdays, and it just happened to be my day on the Saturday the cook did not show up. By the time I arrived, breakfast time was past and the patients had fended for themselves with toast, cold cereal, and orange juice. The other counselor met me on my way in and explained what was happening and that the patients were "pissed off." My response was, "Of course they are. Wouldn't you be?"

I walked into the auditorium to present the morning education lecture, and the tension was so palpable I could almost taste it. If I had ignored this, the patients would not have heard a word I said. So I began by asking, "Okay. What happened with breakfast?" It sounded as though fifty lions roared. Each person began with a piece of the angry tale. Some of the phrases that I was able to pick out of the cacophony were: "We had to make our own." "We couldn't even use the stove." "They treat us like kids." "We're paying hundreds of dollars to be here and this place doesn't care enough to give us a decent breakfast."

You may have noticed that all their words revolved around them as the center of the situation. When they quieted, I said, "Paying as much as you do, I can see why you are so angry. Part of that money is spent for me to present information. So let's start by getting your money's worth on that today. Then we can talk about breakfast." I presented twenty to thirty minutes worth of information on anger. When I was done, I paused, looked at the patients until they were quiet and said, "The cook has never before been late. He has never missed a day. We are afraid something has happened to him. We are putting out extra fruit and snacks in case anyone gets hungry before lunch." I left the auditorium and went to my office. Within five minutes the patient who had been the most vocal showed up. He said, "We hadn't even thought about the cook. When you find out anything, will you let us know?"

There are three guidelines to follow when implementing this technique:

- Do not argue with the angry person. In an argument, the goal is to win, to make the other person the loser. This sets up an adversarial relationship. The longer the argument continues, the greater the emotional investment in not being the loser. Also, the more the other person argues her point, the more she affirms her original beliefs. By participating in an argument, you are actually bolstering her position.
- Use short sentences. Do not go into long explanations. When a person is upset, he listens to the first few words of the stated message and then goes into his own thoughts to figure out his reply. He does not process the rest of the sentence. There is one exception to this. If you make a mistake, the angry individual is likely to hear it, grab on to it, and never let you forget. Long explanations create a higher probability of making a mistake.
- Whenever possible, offer an alternative. If you use the "It's policy" approach described above, are there remedies described in the policy that you can convey to the customer or client? If your agency does not have the services or products that the person is looking for, do you know a place that does? Provide a phone number or address. The whole point of this technique is to show the angry person that you are not the enemy out to get her.

Preparing to Change Interpretations

Take time to prepare before using this technique. Think over your routine days; talk to co-workers. Name the policies that seem to cause the most anger:

Make copies of those policies. If you do not have access to the company policy manual, talk with your supervisor about what you are doing and ask for the copies you need. If policy tends to interfere with common goals a number of clients have, what alternatives can you offer to help them get what they need? What does the client need (phone number, address, appointment, etc.) to access these alternatives? If you do not have the information a customer needs to access an alternative, where can you direct the person to get it?

Client's frustrated goal:

Alternative #1:

Alternative access:

Alternative #2:

Alternative access:

Client's frustrated goal:

Alternative #1:

Alternative access:

Alternative #2:

Alternative access:

Changing the Interpretation

Although I have described the technique of changing the interpretation as a useful tool for responding to customers and clients, it can be just as effectively applied to other relationships, such as those with friends, co-workers, or family members.

People sometimes take things personally even when statements weren't intended that way. Chances are, this is what has occurred if you have a friend who is angry with you and you do not know why. You made a general statement or said something that concerned someone else, and she interpreted it as being directed at her and became angry.

Children especially tend to perceive themselves as the center of the universe. This perception often leads them to blame themselves for situations they have no control over, such as divorce, a relative's death, or a family conflict. They may expect blame from others and act defensively and aggressively to ward it off.

What were three conflicts you have engaged in recently with a friend or family member? What differing or inaccurate interpretation created each conflict? How could you have presented a new interpretation?

First conflict:

Inaccurate interpretation:

New interpretation:

Second conflict:

Inaccurate interpretation:

New interpretation:

Third conflict:

Inaccurate interpretation:

New interpretation:

BEING OF GOOD HUMOR

This technique addresses the internal chemical response. Destructive anger, both aggressive and depressive, is most prevalent during times of extreme tension, moments of panic, or long periods of stress. As explained in chapter 3, adrenaline is produced and released at a faster rate during anxious episodes than during times of calm. If the person in this situation could run away, the hormones would be used up. Since the situation requires the person to stay, anxiety turns to anger and the hormones continue flowing throughout the body.

Another way, besides running or exercise, to counteract the adrenaline of fear and anger is through laughter. Laughing produces endorphins. These hormones ease tension and have a calming effect. This is the opposite of the sensation needed for fear and anger.

It is important when using humor to remember that sarcasm or put-downs trigger the desire for self-protection. After all, *sarcasm* comes from a Greek word that means "to tear flesh." It is an attack and will increase the level of anger. Therefore, the laughter needs to be directed at something not important to the person or at the ridiculousness of the situation or of life in general.

Probably all of us have had an experience that was so ridiculous, or so incongruent with the social setting, that it seemed there was nothing to do but laugh. And the laughter was so strong and so healthy that it lasted for years. An angry episode, because of the tension involved, often ignites this type of humor. That happened for me with a situation that occurred years ago.

A friend and I were invited to dine one Friday night at Mitch and Ellen's house. We looked forward to the meal because Mitch was a professional cook who spent time and effort to prepare food that tasted exquisite. We arrived on time but were quickly informed that Ellen was not home yet. Finally, an hour and a half later, she arrived. Ellen looked, dressed, and sounded like the stereotypical hippie of the 1960s and 1970s. As we helped put the food on the table, Ellen explained she was late because of where she had parked the car. Just as Mitch put the platter of chicken on the table and sat down, he realized that Ellen was informing him that she had parked his beloved Corvette in a fire lane and the police had towed it away. It was impounded on the city lot, unavailable until Monday.

Mitch went ballistic. He ranted and raved about how he couldn't trust her with anything. It was probably dented; the transmission would be shot because of how they towed it. He raised his fist above his head to bang it against the table for emphasis. Instead, he hit the edge of the chicken platter. The platter tilted off the table and sent the chicken across the room. There was tense silence. No one dared breathe. Then I heard Ellen's hippie voice say, "Wow! Did you see that bird fly!" The laughter erupted. It burst from all of us, even Mitch.

I have not seen Mitch or Ellen for about eight years. But my friend and I talk on a regular basis. Whenever one of us is especially irritable or snappish, all the other has to do is mention anything about birds flying for the laughter to start. It helps me keep my life in perspective.

Putting Life Situations into Perspective

Most people who have spent any length of time with another person have shared an experience like the one I described. Often these laughable moments happen during what are considered very important social situations: a first date, a wedding, a funeral, a graduation, meeting the in-laws. Make a list of laughable events from your life, who else was involved, and how it all turned out.

Laughable event:

Other person involved:

How it turned out:

Laughable event:

Other person involved:

How it turned out:

Laughable event:

Other person involved:

How it turned out:

    Many professional people believe that their professionalism requires them to present a serious expression to the customer at all times. I disagree. I believe humor is as important on the job as it is in other social settings. Laughter breaks tension, reduces stress, and deescalates angry feelings.

    A few months ago a sixteen-year-old was in my office ranting about the cigarette smoking restrictions in our facility. I decided to use the technique of providing a new interpretation. I took out my copy of the North Carolina statute on teenage smoking. I put it to my right on my desk and pointed out for him where the applicable pieces of the law were. I even read the section out loud. He grabbed that piece of paper off my desk, hissing, "I don't give a shit what this says." Then he ripped the law to shreds. I quietly watched the little pieces of paper gently flutter to the floor. After they had all landed, I burst out laughing. I looked at the young man, who was staring at me as though I had lost my mind. I said, "John, I do not know how often I have wanted to do that. What did it feel like?"

He replied, "Actually, I'm feeling kind of foolish." Then he started to laugh. The aggression was gone.

I cannot teach anyone how to be humorous nor do I think everyone is capable of being comedic. But I do believe that we all have the capacity to be good-humored. By that I mean to enjoy life, to be willing to laugh at ourselves, and not to take things quite so seriously—in essence, to live life on the verge of laughter.

When we learn to appreciate and enjoy what is around us, including the behaviors of others, our lives become much more enjoyable and much easier to live. Judgments often preempt our appreciation and enjoyment of other people and life events. Some behaviors and life events are very serious and hurtful and need to be judged and taken seriously. Others that involve behaviors or life circumstances that do not create harm or damage can be appreciated and even laughed about. To be good-humored means to know the difference between the serious and the ridiculous, to address the one and enjoy the other, and to do so at work, as well as at home or at play. One way to do this is to stop taking life so seriously.

Enjoying the Outrageous

Customers, clients, co-workers, supervisors, and the supervised can present some outrageous behaviors and circumstances. Instead of complaining and harshly judging them, can you appreciate those behaviors as demonstrations of the ridiculousness of life—not the ridiculousness of the person, but the ridiculousness of the way life and humans are designed?

Think of outrageous behaviors or circumstances that will help you complete the phrases below. Remember the happening as though it is a story. When you have a chance, tell one of the stories to a co-worker.

I once had a customer (patient, client) who

I once had a supervisor who

I once had a co-worker who

    The exercise that you just completed is about enjoying and appreciating human outrageousness. Just before leaving work, I tried the exercise out on a co-worker. I must warn you that it snowballs. At first she had a difficult time thinking of an outrageous incident. Finally, she came up with one. She shared it and we laughed. Her example reminded me of something else. I shared it. We laughed. By then she had another example. Memories of funny events came faster and faster the more we shared and laughed. I hope the same happens for you, because my co-worker and I left work laughing and feeling happy. Because of that, any hardships of the day were left behind.

Taking Ourselves Less Seriously

None of us is exempt from the outrageous and ridiculous. Along with taking life less seriously, we often need to take ourselves less seriously. Whether at home, at the office, or out with friends, there are times for each of us when the sublimely ridiculous occurred. Think of three incidents that have left you saying, "Oh my gosh, I don't believe I did that!" or "Oh my gosh, I don't believe that happened to me!" Give a brief description below and then list whom you could share the stories with.

Oh my gosh, I don't believe

Whom could you share this with?

Oh my gosh, I don't believe

Whom could you share this with?

Oh my gosh, I don't believe

Whom could you share this with?

    Feelings are contagious. When one person is anxious and tense, those nearby become anxious and tense. When a person is happy and enjoying life, others catch that sense of goodwill and playfulness. As you go through life with good humor, enjoying the outrageous behaviors that may occur, family, friends, and customers will respond in kind. The tension in the atmosphere around you will lower and so will the aggressive episodes.

DOING THE UNEXPECTED

Figure D in chapter 4 (page 67) shows that the recipients of destructive anger usually respond by externalizing or internalizing their own angry reactions. The originator of the angry incident expects this to happen. In fact, the hostile individual may be using aggressive or depressive behaviors to elicit either of these response styles from others. And the recipient usually obliges by fighting back verbally or emotionally withdrawing. As long as the originator of this angry interchange receives these expected responses, the destructive anger and hostile words will persist. It is as though both participants have memorized lines of a script.

    One way to stop this cycle is to rewrite your half of the script by responding in an unexpected manner. To accomplish this, you need to discard responses that change the subject (retreat), mete out punishment (retort), berate the other person (retort), or provide a long explanation. These are responses the angry person expects, and they are therefore ineffective. Instead, an aggressive response style needs to be answered with a nondefensive, assertive reply. When done well, this can be an effective response because it does not emotionally trap the other person into fighting back and trips up any replies the aggressor may have rehearsed.

One method of interrupting the anticipated script was skillfully executed in reaction to my anger. I was preparing to present a workshop in a Virginia Beach motel. The motel's servers had set the room up and were still there helping with the last-minute arrangements. I walked in, and the chairs were grouped in a configuration that I find uncomfortable. Annoyed, I snapped at the closest worker, a young woman in her twenties, about the setup. She immediately agreed to get the crew to redo it. A few minutes went by, she said something to me, and I angrily answered. Next she was helping to arrange the snack table and again I made an angry, snappish comment.

The young woman stopped what she was doing, looked at me, and in a very nice tone of voice said, "Excuse me. Have I done something to offend you?" Her response to my boorish behavior took me so by surprise that for a moment I could not think of what to say. Then it hit—I was treating this person badly for no apparent reason and the only civil thing for me to do was to own up to my rudeness and apologize, which I promptly did.

Later that evening I wondered what the young woman would have done if I had said, "Yes, you did offend me." I never had the opportunity to ask her, but having seen how well she responded to me initially, I imagine she might have said something equally skilled, such as, "I didn't mean to. Please, tell me how, so I do not do it again."

Behavioral expressions of anger—such as yelling, standing up and moving toward the target of anger, talking fast, and clenching fists—escalate the internal physiological sensation by increasing the production of adrenaline. The assertive response style offers an effective counter to this phenomenon. Assertiveness is another response to destructively expressed anger that redirects the anticipated script. Because its focus is the Behavior component of the feeling circle, it can help set desired behavioral parameters. The validation of the message and the behavioral aspect of this technique make it especially effective when responding to a young child or an adolescent.

Developing the New Script

Keeping in mind that anger is a method of communication and that the person is attempting to send a message, my first effort when using this technique of developing a new script is to acknowledge my interest in, or the importance of, the message. Next I vocalize the behaviors I need from the other person to help me understand the message. For example:

- "John, I can focus better on what you are saying if you'd sit down."
- "Mary, I want to hear what you are trying to tell me. I can do that only if you lower your voice."
- "Jim, I want to stay and talk about this with you. The only way I will do that is if you stop calling me names."
- "Jan, for me to understand what you are trying to tell me, I need you to slow down."

List three incidents that have involved an angry person. Write a statement that indicates the importance of that person's communication. Then write one that tells how you need the person's behavior to change so that you can hear the communication. Make an assertive statement by combining your communication words with the behavior words.

Incident 1:

Acknowledge the importance of the message:

Describe the behavior change:

Combine the message and behavior statements:

Incident 2:

Acknowledge the importance of the message:

Describe the behavior change:

Combine the message and behavior statements:

Incident 3:

Acknowledge the importance of the message:

Describe the behavior change:

Combine the message and behavior statements:

If you know of someone who tends to be aggressively angry toward you on a regular basis and who acts in a similar style each time, think of how you could implement this method.

Describe the aggressive person's expected behavior:

Acknowledge the importance of the message:

Describe the behavior change:

Combine the message and behavior statements:

During your relaxation session, envision the aggressive person's usual behavior. As that person makes the first aggressive statement:

• Command yourself to STOP.
• Take a deep breath and count to three.
• As you let it out slowly, RELAX.
• Say the assertive statement you developed.

If the statement does not seem comfortable, rework it and try again.

USING EMOTIONAL HONESTY

"My boyfriend yells at me. I feel inadequate and then I can't do anything right."

"Have you told him how you feel?"

"Told him how I feel?"

"Yes. Have you said to him, 'I feel inadequate when you raise your voice and then I make more mistakes.' Have you tried saying that?"

"Well, no. I'm afraid he'll use it against me."

"Use what against you?"

"My feeling."

I have this conversation, or one very close to it, at least five times a week. And each time, it seems that the person responding to my questions peers at me as though I have totally lost my mind for suggesting that any sane human being would even consider divulging personal feelings. There seem to be two strong beliefs held by many in our culture who deem the expression of emotions taboo. One is that when we share our feelings with others, they may use those feelings to manipulate or to blackmail us. The other is that our feelings will offend others. Both of these beliefs are false.

The only way people can be manipulated is through fear or shame. If you come near me with a snake, any kind of snake, and demand something from me, my intense fear of snakes leads me to comply so you will remove that cold-blooded creature. Blackmail, a specific form of manipulation, means promising to keep something hidden to avoid an aversive situation or dishonor. Feelings become instruments of manipulation only when people are afraid of or shamed by their emotions. People who are comfortable with, understand the naturalness of, and attribute positive functions to their feeling states cannot be manipulated or blackmailed through fear or shame of their emotional aspects.

The idea that one person's feelings will offend another person comes from inadequate social training on the differences between thoughts and feelings. A statement such as, "I feel that you do not know what you are doing and you are an idiot," is offensive. It is also not a feeling. That statement, being a judgment, would be more accurate if it began, "I think that you do not know what you are doing." Thoughts consist of opinions, judgments, and attitudes, all of which are arguable, potentially offensive aspects of our Thinking component that open the door to disagreement. There is nothing wrong with disagreements. But when someone is already angry, a disagreement increases the anger within the existing conflict. An aggressive episode, then, is not likely to be defused by expressing brutally honest thoughts.

The use of emotional honesty as a defusion technique can be very effective at reducing destructive behaviors when people are careful to state their feelings rather than thoughts. Using this technique maintains their humanity, alerts the angry person to the effects of the destructive behavior, and highlights an immediate similarity between the people involved.

It goes against nature for most species to hurt or destroy their own members for nonsurvival reasons. The same holds true for humans. The high rate of homicide, violent crime, and war around the world may seem to contradict this concept, but an explanation of what the human brain must do to allow one person to inflict harm on another clears up the discrepancy.

For one person to intentionally hurt another, the mind must be convinced that the harm about to be done is aimed at a thing or animal that is somehow subhuman. This is accomplished by what I call objectification—making a person into an object by the use of negative labeling. These labels make up the languages of prejudice, war, and abuse. Words such as *faggot, gook,* and *whore* take away a person's humanity, make the human being into an object without feelings, and allow the mind to believe that the harm being done is not to one of its own. An emotion expressed in a nonthreatening manner can help remind the aggressor that the person about to be hurt is human.

In about 70 percent of the incidents involving aggression, aggressors are not aware that their behavior has affected other people. Sharing how the angry actions triggered an internal feeling response can alert the aggressor to these emotional effects. At least then the aggressive person has the opportunity to make an informed decision about whether to continue inflicting emotional harm.

In the 1970s, Harvey Hornstein wrote *Cruelty and Kindness,* a book that investigated a number of variables that influence a person's decision to act in an altruistic or aggressive manner.[1] He found that a strong determinant in altruism is the perceived similarity between the helper and the one in need of help. If I happen to be on a pier and see two people, neither of whom I know, drowning and one has on a Tarheels cap, I am more likely to throw him a lifeline first because I would assume that we have something in common, the state where we live. Cross-culturally, feelings are a similarity, a common denominator for all human beings. A society may determine what events create the emotion. Once created, the internal chemical reaction is similar between people.

To employ emotional honesty, we can draw from six of the seven basic emotions: sadness, gladness, guilt, inadequacy, fear, and loneliness. (We'll exclude anger for this technique because it is the feeling designed for fighting. It tends to aggravate, rather than dissipate, the aggression.) By sharing one of these six feelings, we can immediately produce a common characteristic and increase the possibility that the other person will manifest kindness rather than aggression.

Sharing my emotional response and humor are the two techniques I use most often in my personal life. Humor helps to keep life easy and fun, while a potential benefit of sharing my emotions is gaining opportunities to de-velop deeper relationships. Once I became comfortable with my feelings, this defusion technique was easy to use. All it requires is a statement of how I feel about what is happening.

Recently, in a phone conversation with my parents, this technique natu-rally occurred. My mother has Alzheimer's disease, and she responded to me as though she were in another time period. My father became angry and yelled at her. My mom hung up her extension and my dad went on yelling. When he paused, I said, "Dad, I feel sad when I hear you yell at Mom. She can't help it." In a very gruff voice, he responded, "I don't mean to upset you, but . . ." and then he talked on about some of her behaviors. When he paused, I added, "I just wanted you to know how I feel." I heard him take a deep breath. In a soft, sad voice he said, "Sometimes I don't know what else to do." At this point, a host of options opened up—to talk more about my feelings, my father's feelings, or other means of help for my mother.

Some people believe people are aggressive in order to intimidate their victims into doing what they want. They do not want to expose their vul-nerable feelings to these aggressive individuals for fear the aggression will use those feelings as ammunition to intensify their manipulation. Some people use aggression as a problem-solving technique. They often do not know other methods of solving problems.[2] In these situations, there are two things you can do. The first option is to use one of the other five techniques. The second option involves implementing the emotional honesty technique with a minor additional phrase. Share the feeling, let the person know you will still do what needs to be done, and offer another, more productive al-ternative to the aggression. For example, you might say to your supervisor, "I feel inadequate when you yell. If you would point out my mistakes quietly, I'd be able to fix them faster." Or you might say to a customer, "I get ner-vous when you raise your voice like that, and I still have to do my job."

Sharing the Emotion

Inadequacy and fear are the two general categories of feelings that occur when we are confronted with destructively angry response styles. Perhaps synonyms of *afraid*—*anxious, nervous,* or *apprehensive*—are feeling words that might seem easier for you to use. When stating your emotional reaction and its connection to the angry person's expression, avoid using the word *because*. *Because* is easily interpreted as blaming or accusing. These two interpretations increase, rather than defuse, the angry situation.

Think of three separate incidents involving destructive anger. Exactly what did the person say or do? Use the formula shown to label the emotion you felt in response to the person's behavior. If you believe that the person is using aggression to manipulate you, what phrase can you add that indicates your feeling will not change your behavior?

First incident:

I felt _____ when _____ .
Additional phrase(s):

Second incident:

I felt _____ when _____ .
Additional phrase(s):

Third incident:

I felt _____ when _____ .
Additional phrase(s):

Because there are no other feeling words that describe the sensation of inadequacy, some people use thoughts to explain that feeling. As long as the thoughts present the emotion and do not sound accusatory, they can be used safely. For instance, I might say, "I think I'm not important when you don't respond to my suggestions." "I feel like a failure when . . ."

Remember three times when you have felt inadequate. Using thoughts that indicate a sense of inadequacy, complete the formula. Again, complete an additional phrase if you think it will help in your situation.

First incident:

I felt _____ when _____ .
Additional phrase(s):

Second incident:

I felt _____ when _____ .
Additional phrase(s):

Third incident:

I felt _____ when _____ .
Additional phrase(s):

As with the other techniques, this method of defusing aggressive anger will be more available to you if you practice it mentally first. During your relaxation session, envision someone's ire. Command your thoughts to stop. Insert your new response into the mental picture. Rehearse each of the feeling statements above using this method.

The six defusion techniques I have presented in this chapter are not the only methods that will defuse hostile, aggressive situations. Other people have shared with me ways that they respond when they want the anger to dissipate quickly. Those techniques are effective for them, and I encouraged them to continue using them. You may have defusion skills that work well for you. Keep them, use them, and add one or two of the ones I laid out here to them.

I invite you to practice these six defusion techniques. Experiment with them, make them fit your personality, combine them, implement them in a series. The more you examine and test them, the easier they are to use. As long as you remember to present these techniques respectfully, the destructive expression of anger will diminish.

Although the main goal of these techniques is to defuse anger quickly in order to move toward a task-oriented goal, they can also be used to strengthen relationships. This occurs when a defusion technique is used to reduce the wall-building emotion of anger and allow emotions that generate intimacy.

7

Responses to Anger That Open the Door to Emotional Intimacy

THE VERY NATURE OF MONOGAMOUS BONDING requires proximity, relational reflection, and emotional investment. These characteristics of a committed relationship have the potential for igniting intensely angry conflicts.

This morning my dog's territorial behavior reminded me of the intensity that a couple's anger can achieve. I watched my four-legged friend run to the edge of my property, hackles up, barking, while running parallel to a man jogging on the road. My dog's instinct took over and she possessively protected her territory.

When human beings come into close proximity, they tend to do the same. Although creating borders that stake out our personal territory is instinctive, where those borders ought to be and how to protect them is socially defined. Because the individuals forming a relationship come from two different social units, personal boundaries may be different for each, resulting in territorial violations.[1] If the couple does not negotiate the boundary needs of each person, the tendency to aggressively protect individual territory will continue. Another problem that arises with proximity is that the other person is close by, an easy target for misdirected anger.

Relational reflection refers to the natural phenomenon of one person's image reflecting onto the other person or persons in a relational unit.[2] A woman may experience pride in the respect her husband receives from others. A man may take pleasure in the achievements of his wife. A child may brag about a relative's social position as though it enhances her status. In fact, one person may enjoy the other person's success as though it were his or her own, instead of a mere reflection.

132

The potential for anger arises from the possibility that the image reflected will be negative and instead of producing pride, will generate embarrassment. When this happens, individuals may respond as though their own personal image is threatened.

This phenomenon is seen all the time in politics. If a politician's husband is an alcoholic, the campaign managers may struggle to keep that hidden for fear of how it will reflect on their candidate. If the governor's wife has had a number of affairs, how will that make him look? This tendency to catch the reflected image of a partner and incorporate it as part of our own carries the potential that our own esteem may be endangered by that image. Whenever a person perceives a psychic or emotional threat, the fear response is signaled and the protective elements of anger engaged. The person's partner becomes the target of the angry feelings; the person is powerless to change the image and blames the partner for not producing or not changing the image.

The third aspect of a close relationship that has the potential to produce extreme anger is *emotional investment*. If I am walking down the street and a robber demands all my money, I am much less likely to put up a fight when I have two dollars than when I have two hundred dollars in my pocket. How much do I have to lose? How much do I have invested? Usually people join together in a relationship because they care deeply for each other. The relationship fulfills a number of emotional needs, perhaps different for each person, but valuable nonetheless. People involved in a healthy relationship have a lot invested and a lot to lose. Because anger is the feeling designed to defend, whenever an individual senses a threat to the relationship, anger may be activated. Similarly, the other person in a partnership wields the greatest threat to the relationship and to the emotional investment of the first person. Each partner possesses the power to end the relationship by simply walking away. The potential always exists for one partner to betray, abandon, cheat, or in other ways abuse the feelings given to the other partner and to the relationship. If either person perceives this potential threat as an actual threat, the dynamics of anger are quickly set in motion.

Intimacy is the strong state of closeness that results when human beings share vulnerable, meaningful experiences and emotions. On the surface, anger and intimacy seem to be opposites. Intimacy involves closeness while anger creates distance. But surprisingly, they are not opposites; they actually come as a package. Usually, you do not get one without the other. I believe that in a relationship, intimacy is always possible when anger is expressed, especially when it is expressed in productive rather than destructive behaviors. Angry feelings in a healthy partnership indicate vulnerable emotions that need protecting. In a loving couple, anger is not a wall blocking those feelings. It is a closed door, hiding a roomful of sensitivity. Once that door is unlocked and opened, the emotions of intimacy are exposed and available.

Because the emotions protected by anger are vulnerable and sensitive, they are easily bruised. Positive communication skills help to lessen bruising and keep the door of anger open during the sharing process, enabling the intimate event to continue.

At this point, I recommend that you review chapter 5 for a number of effective suggestions that will encourage anger responses that enhance the potential for emotional intimacy.

SECURING THE COMMITMENT

Many happy couples with marital longevity have told me that the first obstacle they had to overcome when responding to an angry partner was the fear of being abandoned. Approximately 90 percent of those I asked had the idea that the relationship could not withstand conflict and heated arguments. They were convinced that their spouse's anger meant he or she was leaving the marriage. Without the reassurance that the partner's anger did not mean desolation of the relationship, they responded by trying to remedy the anger using ineffective response styles such as placating or avoidance. In their minds, they could not risk asserting their needs without jeopardizing the relationship.[3] According to these couples' self-reports, they had to change their misconception to the more accurate understanding that their partners would not leave the relationship just because they experienced an episode of angry feelings. Once this was accomplished, they had the freedom to express their personal feelings and needs.

Write down three reasons that indicate your relationship will not end because your partner feels angry. These explanations can be from historic experience (He got angry last week and he did not leave.) or a direct reassurance by your partner (I told him my fear and he said . . .).

1.

2.

3.

Read out loud the reasons that you listed. Are there more that you have not listed? Think about them one at a time.

ENSURING SAFETY

Once you know the relationship is secure, the next order of business is to establish that there will be no violence—emotional or physical violence. The fear you may feel about potentially dangerous aggression may have nothing to do with your current partner. If your partner has not shown signs of violent behavior when angry, then your expectations of violence, and their accompanying emotional reactions, are rooted in your past, perhaps as far back as your childhood. Such expectations likely originated from repeatedly witnessing angry adults express their feelings with physical and verbal abuse. In fact, there is a strong possibility that you are acting out your gender role, and expecting your partner to act out the other gender role, as those roles were expressed in your family of origin.[4]

This next exercise works best when both partners complete it. If that is not possible, just do the Partner One exercise and skip the Partner Two.

Partner One
In chapter 1 ("What Were Your Initial Lessons?" pages 9–10), you were asked to describe how angry adults interacted when you were a child. Remember or revisit your answers. For this exercise, remember what the angry adults did, how you felt, and what the outcome of the angry incident was. Then

come to your current circumstances, think of two instances when your partner was angry, and answer the questions for each instance.

Describe the first instance:

How did you feel when your partner was angry?

What specific behavior evoked the strongest emotional reaction for you?

What was the outcome of the angry incident?

Describe the second instance:

How did you feel when your partner was angry?

What specific behavior evoked the strongest emotional reaction for you?

What was the outcome of this angry incident?

What would you like the outcome of the next angry incident to be?

Partner Two
Remember a time during your childhood when your primary caregivers were angry with each other. How did you know that at least one was angry? What was said or done?

As you watched or listened to the anger, what were some of your thoughts and how did you feel?

What did you do?

What was the outcome of the angry incident?

Now come to your current circumstances, think of two instances when your partner was angry, and answer the questions for each instance.

Describe the first instance:

How did you feel when your partner was angry?

What specific behavior evoked the strongest emotional reaction for you?

What was the outcome of this angry incident?

Describe the second instance:

How did you feel when your partner was angry?

What specific behavior evoked the strongest emotional reaction for you?

What was the outcome of this angry incident?

What would you like the outcome of the next angry incident to be?

If your answers and your partner's about the next angry incident reflect the desire for a more positive result, perhaps a better understanding of each other or a satisfying resolution to an ongoing conflict, I recommend that you discuss the answers each of you wrote down. Pay especially close attention to the feelings evoked during childhood and their relationship to the emotional reaction triggered by your partner's angry behavioral expressions. You may realize how like your parents you sound even though you have repeatedly said you would handle things differently than they did. Once you have done this, move on to the next exercise together.

CREATING A SAFE, FAIR RELATIONSHIP

People in a partnership need to know that there is safety and an agreement of fairness within the relationship before they can share or listen to angry feelings. To create this safety, guidelines need to be formulated to set limits on conflicts and arguments.[5]

Some guidelines indicate absolutes—those behaviors and subjects that safety and fairness dictate are not acceptable or up for discussion under any conditions. List the absolutes in your relationship. I recommend that the first two be *No physical violence* and *No name calling.*

Time parameters are very helpful in contributing security and fairness. For instance, can an old gripe be brought up weeks later, or is there a statute of limitations? Can new arguments go on forever, or are they limited to twenty-four hours? Some couples have told me that they refuse to go to bed angry, even if it means staying up all night to work things out. What are your time parameters?

Partner One
Are there any angry behaviors listed in the "Ensuring Safety" exercise (pages 135–138) that are especially upsetting to you, behaviors that, if modified, would help you listen more closely to your partner's anger? List them in the order of most upsetting to least upsetting.

Upsetting behavior:

Possible modification: .

Upsetting behavior:

Possible modification:

Upsetting behavior:

Possible modification:

Upsetting behavior:

Possible modification:

Partner Two

Are there any angry behaviors listed in the "Ensuring Safety" exercise that are especially upsetting to you, behaviors that, if modified, would help you listen more closely to your partner's anger? List them in the order of most upsetting to least upsetting.

Upsetting behavior:

Possible modification:

Upsetting behavior:

Possible modification:

Upsetting behavior:

Possible modification:

Upsetting behavior:

Possible modification:

Both Partners
Remember hostile arguments that have occurred with each other. Are there strategies you can implement to evoke a less antagonistic response? These might involve your timing, attitude, or location.

Describe an argument that has occurred:

Strategy to reduce antagonism:

Describe an argument that has occurred:

Strategy to reduce antagonism:

Describe an argument that has occurred:

Strategy to reduce antagonism:

DEVELOPING THE FAIRNESS TENET

Responding to angry expressions in a way that exposes the vulnerable feelings that reside beneath the anger requires each partner to believe in the
fairness of the other person. Each individual must believe deeply that even
during the most heated conflicts and disagreements, the basic tenet of fairness will guide the other throughout the verbal altercation and the fairness
within each partner will prevail to produce a solution that is just and equitable for both of you.[6]

Partner One

Describe three instances when your partner has demonstrated fairness:

1.

2.

3.

Describe three incidents when you have demonstrated fairness to your partner:

1.

2.

3.

Partner Two

Describe three instances when your partner has demonstrated fairness:

1.

2.

3.

Describe three incidents when you have demonstrated fairness to your partner:

1.

2.

3.

Your relationship may have a history of unfair fighting. Perhaps the anger ignites and expands so quickly that someone loses control and you or your normally fair partner resorts to dubious tactics to win arguments. If this is the case, you need to find ways to slow the escalation and to stop the unfair practices. The first step in this process is to identify problem behaviors.

What actions have occurred during previous conflicts that you and your partner agree are unfair?

Unfairness by Partner One:

Unfairness by Partner Two:

In the heat of an argument, people sometimes forget or ignore the agreed-upon guidelines and unfair practices. You and your partner can use certain techniques to slow the escalation of the argument:

- Implement one of the defusion techniques from chapter 6. This will pause the unfair outburst long enough to re-initiate the safety and fairness guidelines.
- Develop a gesture or verbal cue that you both will recognize as a signal to stop, take a deep breath, and slow down when something unfair occurs.
- Each of you presents your side of the conflict using paper and pen. No matter how fast you can write, it is slower than talking. When done writing, cross out the aspects of your message that violate the agreed-upon guidelines and the fairness tenet. When you are finished, read the remainder to your partner.

ENSURING EQUALITY

An egalitarian partnership provides the most effective forum for the healthy expression of anger, resolution of conflict, and development of intimacy.[7] It does not matter what specific purpose the anger might serve in a specific instance—whether to communicate, protect, or bring about change. The core function can be seen as an attempt to equalize power. Figure B in chapter 3 (page 49) and figures C and D in chapter 4 (pages 56 and 67) demonstrate this phenomenon. The Emotion and Thought areas above the dotted line consist of feelings and thoughts characteristic of vulnerability and weakness, indicating a state of powerlessness. The Emotion and Behavior areas below this line, composed of anger and its potential expressions, are displays of strength, indicating a state of power.

The external exhibition of power is meant to compensate for the internal sensation of limited power. When both people in a relationship perceive themselves and the other as equals, the energy involved in anger does not need to compensate for the perceived or real imbalances between partners.

Egalitarianism in a relationship assists in the healthy expression of anger by inhibiting aggressive behavior. Remember, aggression usually flows from a person with greater power toward one with lesser power. Perhaps at work your supervisor calls you into her office and lays into you for making errors in your work. Most people in your position would not respond aggressively, and you probably would not, either. Instead, you leave her office, sputtering and muttering to yourself or to a friend about the unfair criticism.

Later that day, as you take the bus home, you continue to replay the scene. By the time you reach home, your anger has grown to ten times the volume it was upon exiting her office. You cast a glance at your twelve-year-old's room as you head to your bedroom to change clothes. You see his room again as you walk by on your way to the kitchen, where you are hit with the sight of dishes in the sink and unfinished food on plates still sitting out on the counter. Your anger flares. Just then your son walks in and you verbally let him have it. You ream him out for his room and the kitchen, judging him harshly and critically for his inadequacy in performing as a member of your family. Your words are cutting and hurtful.

Aggression flows downward from the person with more power to the one with lesser power, like water running down a decline. To stop the flow of the water, you would have to bring in a bulldozer and regrade the land until it is level. In a relationship, to reduce the issue of destructively expressed anger, we level the power so there are limited imbalances.

In the following exercise, mark each category in which you see yourself as not being equal to your partner. Notice that your perception is being requested. This is much more important than the actuality because your interpretation of the situation affects your anger and response to a far greater extent than the reality. For the areas where you indicate inequality, explain how you decided there was disparity.

Person One

Power Base	Not Equal	Explanation
Education		
Social status		
Finances		
Self-expression		
Final decisions		
Parenting responsibility		
Family cohesion		
Household responsibility		
House maintenance		

Person Two

Power Base	Not Equal	Explanation
Education		
Social status		
Finances		
Self-expression		
Final decisions		
Parenting responsibility		
Family cohesion		
Household responsibility		
House maintenance		

Inspect both charts. Do they indicate equality? Equality does not have to be in the same area. One person may have greater education, while the other has access to more financial resources. Also, some categories may be considered more important by a couple than other categories. The person who functions higher in an important category is bestowed more power than the partner who functions higher in a category of lesser importance.

If the charts show a gross imbalance, what can you do to create a more equitable relationship? Some disparities cannot be remedied immediately. In fact, some may not be changeable at all. Do not look at shuffling or enhancing category by category. Instead, look at groups of categories or the relationship as a whole and ask, "What would make us equals in this partnership?" Write your answers down.

Implement this new arrangement for two weeks. Then revisit your solution. Are there still gross inequities?

How can these be renegotiated?

If you discover that one area throws the power out of balance for some time, such as attaining a college degree, discuss the length of time, expected shift of power, and any compensatory methods to maintain power equilibrium for the expected duration of the imbalance.

Length of time expected:

Shift of power:

Compensatory methods:

SIFTING THROUGH THE GARBAGE

Imagine that, by mistake, you threw away a valued piece of jewelry. It is somewhere in the large green trash bag that you were just about to take out for tomorrow morning's garbage pickup. When you realize where that important trinket has come to repose, your heart sinks, a few nasty words fly through your mind (maybe even escape from your lips), and you shrug your shoulders. Nothing can be done except to begin working on the messy task at hand—sifting through the garbage to find the gold.

Responding to your partner's anger has many similarities to this jewelry hunt. Your dominant lessons about anger and its expression may have been so negative and confusing that anger and its triggers are hidden among the garbage of inconsequential situations and fictitious targets. They camouflage the anger's purpose and the reactions beneath the angry feelings. When this happens, anger cannot function productively because the people in the relationship do not know what really triggered the anger. Once the situation and target are clarified, you can reach the more vulnerable feelings that the anger has been defending. Only then does intimacy develop.

The following exercises are designed to promote responses to anger that focus on relevant subjects, investigate the thoughts and emotions beneath the angry expressions, and encourage more meaningful levels of emotional exchange.

Finding the Essence

John arrived home from work early. He was on the computer, looking up baseball statistics, when he heard Elaine's car pull into the driveway. He shut down the computer and went to the kitchen to greet his spouse. She was already in the kitchen, staring at the stove. John's eyes followed his wife's gaze to the half-eaten ham, left uncovered and spoiling, since yesterday's dinner. Janna, their teenage daughter, had forgotten to wrap it up and put it in the refrigerator. Elaine started to rant about the ham, how it was spoiled, how the kids had no sense of responsibility—the least they could do to help out was put food away—and she went on until she had to pause for breath. At that point, John asked, "What's the essence?"

Elaine, not one to be easily redirected, spit back, "What do you mean, what is the essence? Janna wasted half a ham. THAT'S THE ESSENCE!"

John replied, "I can understand you being angry about that. It doesn't call for this much anger. What is the essence, the core, of what's going on?"

Elaine's angry energy lessened enough that she was willing to listen to her husband. She mentally reviewed her day. She had spent most of the time worrying about her company's cash flow and her family's personal finances. Eight hours of financial anxiety was bundled together, turned into anger, and thrown at that wasted ham. Nothing can be done about the spoiled ham. Financial threats, on the other hand, present situations that John, Elaine, and even their teenage daughter can strategize about together.

The word *essence* is John's. It fits his personality. Jokingly, he calls himself "a New Age sensitive guy." Even though he says this with a chuckle, I think he means it. The word he chose in the anecdote works for him, although it might not for you. Fortunately, the specific wording doesn't matter. What does matter is understanding that the target of angry feelings has not always provoked the anger. Learning to present that idea spontaneously, comfortably, and in a practical way when the other person is verbalizing intense feelings is the goal.

Think of two ways you can ask your partner what the anger is about.

1.

2.

Imagine two previous incidents when your partner seemed angrier than the situation demanded.

First incident:

Second incident:

During your daily relaxation session, when you are very relaxed:

- Imagine the first incident.
- As you mentally replay it, find an appropriate spot and insert your first question.
- Then do this process again, inserting your second question.

Sometimes people can help their partners find the essence of their anger by suggesting potential stressors. For example, John could have asked Elaine: "What is this anger really about? Are there still cash-flow problems at your company?"

A minimally risky way to experiment with this method of responding is to think of an angry incident far enough removed in time that your partner is no longer sensitive to the situation. Then answer the following questions:

What was the angry situation?

What was the target of the anger?

What is your "essence" of anger question?

What do you suspect the anger was really about?

Bring the incident up to your partner and ask if your suspicion is true. If your partner denies having another motive for the anger or says that your suspicions are not correct, do not insist that you are right. Let it drop. The more you insist, the more resistance you will meet.

MANAGING STRESSORS TOGETHER

If anger seems to be in greater abundance today than in the past, there may be a number of stressors impinging upon the security of your relationship. One way to increase the potential for intimacy, as well as to reduce threats and the anger evoked to fight them, is to work together on plans for managing these stressors.

With your partner, carefully review the list below. Indicate which areas have active stressors by specifying the problem that is producing the stress.

Employment:

Financial:

Parental:

Social:

Legal:

Medical:

Familial:

Relational:

Other:

As you go through the areas on the list, discuss the specifics of each stressor. Agree on what the exact problem is for each. Together, choose the one that seems to cause the most problems. Develop a plan either to remedy the problem or to reduce the stress it generates.

Identify the exact problem generating the stress:

What are the steps that need to be taken, and who needs to be responsible for each step? If you are unsure of what can be done about your stressful situation, your first step is to call someone who knows how your problem can be solved.

Do we need to call someone, and if so, whom?

Plan of Action
Step 1:

Performed by

No later than

Step 2:

Performed by

No later than

Step 3:

Performed by

No later than

Step 4:

Performed by

No later than

If circumstances change or the problem becomes worse instead of better, call that person who knows more about the problem again. Do not hesitate to seek assistance. There is no shame in asking for help.

OPENING THE DOOR TO INTIMACY

A dinner served fifteen minutes late, a yard mowed to less than perfection, or clothes forgotten at the cleaners are not normally mishaps that have enough consequences to provoke extreme anger. When a partner overreacts to mistakes such as these, there is more affecting that person's interpretation of the events. Intimate relationships often cultivate the negative self-messages planted in childhood because the interconnected nature of the emotional bond extends these messages to the entire relationship.

When two people come together as a couple, each brings a unique personal identity. In the relationship, these two identities connect to form a third identity. This connection creates an image of the relationship as a unit in itself. The negative self-messages from both people are now a part of this new entity, and as a result, each partner may interpret events as a direct evaluation of the relationship and as an indirect evaluation of the partners within that relationship. In other words, "When you do something stupid, then we are seen as stupid." Someone who has a strong negative self-message of intelligence, might think, "When you do something stupid, it reflects on the relationship as stupid, which means that I am stupid."

Each participant in the partnership has a dynamic process of valuing and devaluing himself or herself within the context of the relationship. Whether a behavior by one participant values or devalues the image of the relationship, and hence the other person within that relationship, depends on that person's self-messages and how those messages help interpret the partner's action.

Responding to anger created as a reflection of the relationship's image is a five-step process:

1. Listen carefully. You know that anger is the emotion, and you know the event. Now listen for what that event might have meant to your partner. Is the event seen as a betrayal, a letdown, an embarrassment?

2. Clarify what you think you have heard. Using words that fit your personality and your rhythm of speech, ask if what you think your partner is saying is really what is being said. You can ask this one of two ways. The first way acknowledges the anger: "Are you angry because you think I let you down?" This method of clarification is useful when your partner is aware of the anger.

   If your partner is pouting and sullen, pointing out anger may not help. Simply leave the anger out of the question and ask, "Do you think I let you down?"

3. Listen to the answer and then reflect the feeling. If your partner says you still don't understand, ask for more information: "Okay, what were you trying to say?" Once you are given more information, clarify that. Once you both agree that you understand what your partner has said, validate the feeling: "I feel angry too when I think someone has let me down."

4. Negate irrational perceptions: "I can see how you thought you were let down. That was not my intent."

5. Encourage intimacy by sharing. Again, you have two possible options. You can share a similar experience that happened to you and how you reacted. Or, you can share how you feel in response to your partner's information. If you decide on the second option, choose a feeling and way to express it that is not judgmental or accusatory.

Remember an incident when you thought that your partner had reacted with anger that seemed extreme for the situation. Replay the incident in your mind, and then use the five-step process to determine responses that have the potential to generate intimacy.

Step 1: What might the trigger event mean to your partner?

Step 2: What question would clarify that information?

Step 3: How could you validate your partner's feeling?

Step 4: How could you negate the interpretation?

Step 5: Write down a similar personal experience and your reaction.

Think of another incident and follow the same process as you did with the first.

Step 1: What might the trigger event mean to your partner?

Step 2: What question would clarify that information?

Step 3: How could you validate your partner's feeling?

Step 4: How could you negate the interpretation?

Step 5: How do you feel in response to your partner's interpretation?

WALKING THROUGH THE DOOR TO INTIMACY

Self-messages not only cast distorted reflections of the relationship image onto the participants, they also interfere with how participants interpret daily events. The most persistent negative self-messages are those that almost everyone has, to one extent or another—messages that question our adequacy, importance, and worth. These are very sensitive messages because they compose the core of a person's shame. Being so sensitive, they are tightly and often passionately defended by anger.

It is not easy to penetrate the wall of defenses that keep others out. One method that might encourage your partner to reveal his or her hurtful self-messages is for you to be the first to tear down the wall and share the negative messages that undermine your self-esteem and distort how you interpret events.

Complete the sentences below using incidents from your relationship. These incomplete sentences are most effective if both participants in the relationship do a set of their own. Fill in all of the available sentences, even if you struggle to remember enough situations to do so.

Partner One

I think I am not important when

I think I am not important when

I think I am not important when

I think I am not good enough when

I think I am not good enough when

I think I am not good enough when

Partner Two

I think I am not important when

I think I am not important when

I think I am not important when

I think I am not good enough when

I think I am not good enough when

I think I am not good enough when

When you and your partner complete these sentences, share your answers with each other. Do this in a nonaccusatory way. Remember, you did not create each other's negative self-messages; they have been affecting your lives for many years before you even met each other. The significant point for both of you to understand is that these are ways that you sometimes think about yourselves, and the behaviors you have written down tend to trigger these thoughts.

Negative self-messages are irrational statements that lead us to misinterpret behaviors. Therefore, the next important task is for each of you to look at the triggering events. Did your partner intend for you to interpret the triggering behavior the way you did? Look at your list. For each sentence, one at a time, ask your partner if that is what was intended. For example, "Did you want me to think I am unimportant when . . . ?" or "Did you want me to think I am not good enough when . . . ?"

The next important task is for each of you to determine which behaviors you are willing to modify and devise a cue to help each other remember to use the modifications. Look at your partner's list and determine which behaviors you are willing to change and how you are willing to change them. What gesture or verbal cue will remind you to use the new behavior?

Partner One

Triggering behavior:

Modification: _____ Cue: _____

Triggering behavior:

Modification: _____ Cue: _____

Triggering behavior:

Modification: _____ Cue: _____

Triggering behavior:

Modification: _____ Cue: _____

Triggering behavior:

Modification: _____ Cue: _____

Triggering behavior:

Modification: _____ Cue: _____

Partner Two
Triggering behavior:

Modification: _____ Cue: _____

Triggering behavior:

Modification: _____ Cue: _____

Triggering behavior:

Modification: _____ Cue: _____

Triggering behavior:

Modification: _____ Cue: _____

Triggering behavior:

Modification: _____ Cue: _____

Triggering behavior:

Modification: _____ Cue: _____

If you did the beginning part of this exercise alone, you can still share your completed sentences with your partner. Choose a time when you know your partner will be conducive to listening and talking. Using words that are comfortable for you, share a time when you thought you were not important. Ask for a time when your partner has had a similar thought. In fact, you might begin the conversation by asking, "Are there any times when I did something and you had the thought that you weren't important?"

For people in an intimate relationship, hurtful self-evaluations generate the fear that their partner will stop caring and loving. Fear makes them hypervigilant to environmental cues that might signal the threat. They become compelled to evaluate their partner's actions by looking for behavioral cues that indicate whether their partner still loves and cares for them. People in this situation make statements such as, "If you cared about me, you'd have dinner ready when I get home" or "If you loved me, you'd make sure the toilet seat is left down." Dinners at a certain time and toilet seats down might be signs of consideration, but they are not necessarily signs of caring or love. When someone says these sentences, or ones similar to them, an accurate accompanying feeling statement would be "I am afraid you don't love me" or "I am afraid you don't care about me."

When your partner utters, "If you love me you'd . . ." "If you care you'd . . ." or a similar phrase, take a deep breath and practice the quick relaxation technique that you learned in chapter 5. As your physiology slows down, you can choose between at least two options: clarification ("Do you really think I don't love you because . . . ?") or direct communication ("I want you to know that my love for you is more important than . . .").

If you and your partner are completing the exercises in this book together, the following one can be a springboard for emotionally intimate dialogue. It asks each of you to identify times when you have thought the demanding, angry phrase that begins, "If you . . . me, you'd . . ." and then replace it with an accurate fear statement.

Partner One

If you _____me, _____ you'd _____

_____ .

I am afraid you don't _____ me when_____

_____ .

If you _____ me, _____ you'd _____

_____ .

I am afraid you don't _____ me when_____

_____ .

If you _____me, _____ you'd _____

_____ .

I am afraid you don't _____ me when_____

_____ .

Partner Two

If you _____ me, _____ you'd _____
_____ .

I am afraid you don't _____ me when_____
_____ .

If you _____ me, _____ you'd _____
_____ .

I am afraid you don't _____ me when_____
_____ .

If you _____ me, _____ you'd _____
_____ .

I am afraid you don't _____ me when_____
_____ .

Share a fear statement with your partner. Ask your partner to describe how he or she feels when listening to your fear. Respond to your partner's statement by sharing your reciprocal feeling. Do any behaviors need to change to help address the feelings shared by either of you? If so, then you may need to negotiate how they will change.

Complete the exercise by sharing each of the fear statements separately, following the process delineated above.

CLOSING THE DOOR ON JEALOUSY

Jealousy is a unique emotional state. It consists of a number of feelings, most often occurs in a sexual relationship, involves an element of competition, and must have a third entity present in order to exist.[8] Jealousy, in and of itself, is not an emotion. It is a state of being that involves three of the basic feelings—anger, fear, and sadness—any one of which can be dominating the internal reaction at a given point in time. Because of the fear and the intense, protective anger that jealousy can inundate a relationship with, it is appropriate to address certain aspects of this emotional state here.

The major difference between the anger of jealousy and the anger discussed earlier in this chapter is that jealousy involves competition with a rival that is viewed as a threat to the relationship. The rival most often is another person, but it can also be the partner's job, hobby, or participation in a sport. The irony is that the emotional state of jealousy exists to protect the relationship, but the behaviors most often used to express that jealousy tend to have harmful effects on the relationship.

In fact, some people become so consumed with jealousy that they exhibit the extreme destructive behaviors that express anger. They have the potential to severely, even fatally, harm themselves or people around them. According to authors Annmarie Cano and K. Daniel O'Leary, jealousy is the most common motive cited in the United States for homicide of a wife.[9] A person whose jealousy is this intense needs to seek professional assistance. If this person is your partner and refuses to go for professional counseling, then you need to go for that help because you may have some very difficult choices to make, especially if your safety is at risk.

There are two other situations involving your partner's jealousy for which I would encourage you to consider professional counseling. The first is if the jealous reaction is appropriate in light of your behavior. For instance, if you are in a committed, monogamous relationship and you are having, or have had, an affair, then assistance is important to investigate the motivating factors for the affair and to sort through the emotional residue that both you and your partner carry from the affair. The other situation that indicates the need for couple's counseling is if you are purposefully trying to generate a jealous reaction in order to manipulate your partner. Manipulation is a covert, immature style of communication. It is at odds with a healthy relationship, which depends on open, direct interactions to engender trust between partners.

Identifying Specific Jealousy-Producing Events

If jealousy arises when an event is innocent or neutral, the first task is to identify the specific behaviors that elicit that reaction. The information requested in this exercise will be more accurate if your partner is willing to help you develop it.

In the past month, when has your partner experienced jealousy? What were the exact words your partner said during each of those incidents?

Jealous incident:

Exact words:

Jealous incident:

Exact words:

Jealous incident:

Exact words:

Jealous incident:

Exact words:

Responding Positively to Jealous Accusations

Although it is difficult to respond positively to a criticizing partner, studies indicate that jealousy, like destructive anger, is generated from low self-worth. Becoming trapped in a response pattern similar to the one displayed by figure D (see page 67) reduces relationship satisfaction and increases the intensity of the jealous reaction. There are two positive methods that are more likely to produce productive responses. The first highlights your partner's personal qualities. For example, "I would not trade your tenderness for anything he has to offer." The second method focuses on the value you place on the partnership. For example, "Our marriage is too important for me to risk it by what you suggest."

It is important that you are honest and sincere when choosing your partner's qualities and the relationship value because your partner may accuse you of using these statements as manipulative lies. If that happens, do not argue. I recommend that you either restate your positive response using different words or revisit the defusion techniques. In this type of situation, emotional honesty can be most advantageous. The important point is to remain positive. These responses will not immediately dissipate the jealousy, but over time, they change the emotional atmosphere in such a way that the jealousy weakens and relationship offers greater satisfaction for both partners.

The next task is for you to determine a positive response to the accusations made. In both of the examples I gave, I used a vague phrase for the accusation. As you construct your responses, replace my vagueness with the exact accusation you listed above.

Jealous incident:

Personal quality response:

Value of partnership response:

Jealous incident:

Personal quality response:

Value of partnership response:

Jealous incident:

Personal quality response:

Value of partnership response:

Jealous incident:

Personal quality response:

Value of partnership response:

Negotiating a Compromise

Another behavioral response to jealousy is to negotiate a compromise. I must give a word of caution about compromising. Make sure you are willing to modify the behavior you are negotiating. If the current behavior is important to you, then modifying it is likely to create a resentment that will harm the relationship. When that's the case, you may prefer to be assertive and maintain the behavior. Be honest with yourself as you evaluate each situation's importance.

If you do decide you are willing to modify the behavior through compromise, then know how much of a change you are willing to tolerate.

Looking at the previous list of jealousy-evoking situations, which are you willing to modify, and what are your limits of modification?

Behavior to be compromised:

Limits of modification:

Behavior to be compromised:

Limits of modification:

Behavior to be compromised:

Limits of modification:

Behavior to be compromised:

Limits of modification:

Practice how you can approach your partner to begin negotiations by writing out what you will say. For example, you could start the conversation by saying, "I know it upsets you when I. . . . Let's work out a compromise."

As you practice the methods of responding to your partner that are outlined in this chapter, you will notice that arguments become fewer and less intense. When this happens, communication within your partnership will increase, resulting in greater relationship satisfaction for both of you.

8

Positive Responses to Children's Anger

SITUATED WITHIN THE VALLEY OF OAXACA IN MEXICO, there are two Zapotec communities, La Paz and San Andres. These two communities are similar in location, racial ancestry, population, religion, and location. Even their stated values of respectfulness toward others, equality of all individuals, and social cooperation are the same. But there is one major difference between these two groups that has a dramatic influence on each person's sense of safety: their attitudes about and responses to physical aggression.[1] In San Andres:

- Unruly, rambunctious behavior by children is considered the nature of children.
- Corporal punishment is a common way of disciplining children.
- Fighting is thought of as a natural part of male childhood.
- Physical altercations are common between teenagers, adult men, and spouses.
- Killing another person is understandable, if not acceptable, under certain conditions.

While in La Paz:

- Parents expect their children will behave positively.
- Physical discipline of children is not heard of. Discipline consists of verbal instructions, demonstrations, and supervision.
- Fighting among children is not acceptable.
- Rarely are physical bouts seen among teenagers, adult males, and

spouses. These rare occurrences are met with harsh gossip and disapproval.

- Killing another human being is socially unacceptable under any circumstances.

As the San Andres children grow up, they become more and more aggressive. Play fighting turns into dangerous brawls by the time they reach
adolescence. The adults in this community have a homicide rate of 18.1 per
100,000 persons per year.

Most of the children of La Paz remain nonaggressive throughout their
childhood, into and through adolescence, and on to adulthood. There are
3.4 homicides for every 100,000 people per year.

Where would you want to raise your child? Given the choice, would
you prefer the potentially violent community of San Andres or the mostly
peaceful environment provided by La Paz?

Some of you are probably thinking that these questions are unfair, that
the violence permeating many sectors of our society makes it impossible to
choose safety for our children. Because violence seems to be a part of the
culture, however, does not mean you cannot prepare your child for a nonviolent life. The first experience of a community is the home. You can choose
to establish yours as a violence-free place to live.

As you read through this chapter, you may be surprised that some common methods of responding to children's anger are not included. I do not
encourage punishment. Punishment often carries an element of humiliation
and almost always instills a greater experience of powerless rage. I am un-
conditionally against hitting of any kind, including spanking. Any type of
hitting teaches the child that problem solving can be done aggressively, and
bigger, stronger people can hit others without consequences.

I likewise do not support rewarding a child for good behavior. Good
behavior is an expectation in my world. Mild praise for a job well done and
a thank-you is enough. Otherwise the youngster learns to produce for external gratification. When the rewards stop, so does the positive behavior.

I am not a proponent of time-outs. I think that the time-out technique is
more for the adult's benefit, providing adults time to control their own anger
at the expense of the child's esteem and self-confidence. It has never made
sense to me that people want to remove a child from a social setting by placing her in isolation in order to teach her how to act in a social setting.

Discipline is a word that comes to us from Latin, and it means "to teach." This chapter will help you discover methods to teach your youngster frustration management and conflict resolution that do not involve the techniques described above. Also it will assist you in responding to your child's anger in ways that validate the feeling, while directing the angry emotion toward productive ends. The cost to you is time. And for your child, the most valuable commodity that you can give is time.

By observing La Paz and San Andres, anthropologists have found that what the youngster learns in one developmental stage is carried into and influences the next stage. This is true for children in all cultures. An infant who develops self-soothing techniques will be more compliant and follow directions better when a toddler. The preschooler who internalizes the basic behaviors of self-assertion will not be bullied when old enough to attend elementary school. And the school-aged child who learns how to make sound decisions will be less likely to impulsively act out a violent deed as a preadolescent.

This chapter is divided into four developmental stages. The ages indicating upper and lower limits for each stage are approximations. Some children enter and leave a stage sooner than indicated, others later, and still others right on the mark. The important point is that certain developmental tasks need to take place in each stage. While these tasks are occurring, caregivers can provide positive direction that will guide the child in productively expressing angry feelings.

INFANCY (BIRTH TO TWO YEARS)

Babies' days are filled with more activity than that involved in eating, sleeping, and demanding a regular change of diapers. There are many developmental tasks they need to master in the initial two years of life.[2] The tasks necessary for a baby's emotional development can be classified as social interaction, self-regulation, affect differentiation, and self-possession. Within each category are parental interventions that benefit the infant's affective development as it relates to the expression and use of anger.

A baby begins *social interaction* efforts within the first six months of life while a bond forms between the infant and the primary caregiver, usually the mother. From this relationship and the immediate environment, the child needs to obtain a sense of emotional safety that is strong enough to develop trust in the surrounding world and its inhabitants. The security cultivated during the initial social interactions will influence the child's interpretation of events, and hence the production of destructive and constructive anger, for at least the next three developmental stages.

During the first twelve months, the interaction between mother and child consists of affective displays and affective responses. The baby cannot talk, his or her first word will not be uttered until around the twelfth month, and specific, meaningful gestures are unknown. But the early infant can show happiness, sadness, anger, and surprise. By displaying and responding with these emotions, mother and child develop an active two-way system of communication. It is through this emotional structure that the immensely important trust and security is built.[3] To assist this process, caregivers can:

- Provide a soothing atmosphere, especially during the first two or three months, by playing soft music and speaking in soft tones.
- Speak to the infant using feeling words that match your affect. If you are smiling and happy, talk about being happy. If you are sad, tell your baby you feel sad.
- Refrain from emotionally lying. If you are tense and upset, do not go to the crib, pick your child up, and put a fake smile on your face. The happy face is not congruent with your emotion. The baby senses this and becomes confused.

During the first two months, infants spend a good deal of time practicing *self-regulation*.[4] They are attempting to find the balance between over- and understimulation. As children become more interactive with caregivers and other adults, they exert effort at self-regulation to reduce the stimulation generated by two general states of being, pleasure and distress. If a caregiver ignores a baby's behavioral signals that indicate a need to self-regulate, the overstimulation, caused by the pleasurable activity, remains high and is experienced by the child as distress.

I was visiting a friend who has a nine-month-old baby. She and the infant were playing a game similar to peek-a-boo. She would place a thin handkerchief over her face, and just as the child would reach to grab it, she would blow enough air out of her mouth to send the cloth up, and quickly she would say, "Surprise." The child would laugh, and her mom would hug her and do it all over again. After the third sequence, the baby sat back, turned slightly away, put her thumb in her mouth, stared off, and made a sucking sound. At that point, mom also sat back, taking the break to continue her conversation with me. Her infant was left to self-regulate and self-comfort by thumb-sucking and emotional withdrawal. Other mothers have told me that their infants managed stimulation in other ways besides thumb-sucking. For instance, one child self-comforted by rubbing her mother's elbow.

No matter how the infant calms herself, it is important that the adults who are present do not interfere. If a well-meaning caregiver attempts to gain the baby's attention by making noises or bringing her face close to the child's, the infant will turn farther away and probably show distress. If the caretaker does not take the hint and continues being intrusive, the infant may become more distressed, even displaying anger, and is likely to push at the adult's face to make it go away. A continuous pattern of this type of intrusion into the baby's attempts at self-calming will reduce his ability to relieve stimulation and to provide self-comfort.

Another common form of distress that arises during the child's first two years is caused by frustration. An infant's ability to accomplish physical tasks is extremely limited. Spying a favorite toy just out of his reach, he cannot get it. He is frustrated. He feels angry. He fusses. The day comes when he can crawl around on the floor. Unfortunately, that favorite toy has somehow made it to the coffee table. He heads over in that direction. He gets to the table. He is not strong enough to pull himself up. Again he is frustrated. He feels angry. He fusses. He cries. Finally, he plops down, puts his thumb in his mouth, and gazes off at nothing. He is again self-soothing in order to regulate the internal overstimulation.

This scene could end a little differently. As he is frustrated by not being able to achieve his goal, he begins to fuss. His eye catches sight of the red ball near the couch. He is distracted from his original goal and makes a bee-line toward the ball. His original mission and concurrent frustration are forgotten.

There is an immediate benefit in knowing how to respond to your infant when she is fussing and angry as a result of frustration. Because an infant has many limitations, frustration is a common occurrence. There may be a long-term benefit in knowing how to react to your baby during frustrating episodes. Recent research indicates that infants (tested at seven months old) who can regulate the stimulation generated by frustration, are more likely, when they reach two and a half years old, to follow parental directions than infants who cannot self-regulate.[5] An infant has two main methods of reducing the effects of frustration, and there are simple responses that you can use to help. I recommend that you do not use one to the exclusion of the other because it is preferable that your infant has a number of skills to regulate internal stimulation.

- Self-regulation requires the infant to soothe and calm herself. As a caregiver, you can assist the infant in developing this ability by backing off, allowing the child to initiate self-comforting techniques.
- Distraction redirects the infant's attention away from the goal that is beyond his reach and toward an object or activity that is available to him. This may require you to provide a distracting object that will draw your baby's attention. Given time and greater cognitive development, your infant will learn to seek out his own distractions to reduce the internal effects from experiencing frustration.
- Words said in a soothing tone of voice help to calm infants and early toddlers. Removal or reduction of sensory stimulation such as bright lights or loud music can facilitate the child's attempts at self-calming.

Self-regulation addresses the Chemical area of the feeling circle. The infant learns to control her internal physiological reaction by practicing behaviors that reduce the causative chemicals.

Moving along the feeling circle, the next areas are the Emotion and then the Behavior components. In the infancy period of development, *affect differentiation* is connected to both these areas. Babies learn to recognize and identify different emotions according to how they appear and how they sound. At least two recent research projects have shown that seven-month-old infants demonstrate the ability to distinguish the grossly different feelings of angry and happy, as well as more closely allied emotions such as happy and interested. Familiarity is the determining factor in an infant's recognition of specific feelings. Sad is the emotion identified the fewest times by babies and the emotion expressed the least by infants' parents. The emotion babies recognize the next fewest times is anger, also expressed the next fewest times by their caretakers.[6]

It is important that children learn to recognize, label, and express feelings in ways that enable their emotions to function effectively. For this to occur, they need to know what each feeling is called (Emotion area) and how each feeling looks when expressed (Behavior area). This requires social instruction by the primary caregiver, the first agent of socialization. Familiarity with each feeling is the key factor for infants when identifying and differentiating the various emotions. Repetition of facial and vocal expression socializes the infant to each feeling's socially acceptable form of communication. Below are some suggestions on implementing this socialization process.

- During the first six months, facial expressions of emotional reactions guide the infant. Focus on the four basic emotions of mad, glad, sad, and afraid. Show these feelings facially using an exaggerated affective display. Try to give equal time to each feeling. Remember, if you slight a feeling, then your infant will have a more difficult time recognizing that emotion.
- Throughout infancy, read to your infant stories that have characters with emotions. If you are reading a story that does not specifically identify a feeling, add it in as an aside. The little pig that had his house blown away probably felt afraid and then angry and then sad. Little Red Riding Hood surely felt intense fear when she finally realized that her life was in danger. With the right timing and exaggerated emotional expression, babies often end up enjoying the feeling sidebars as much as, if not more than, the story.
- From around eighteen months to two years, your child's vocabulary and word usage become larger and more complex. At the end of this developmental stage, your infant will know a hundred words or more. Only four of those hundred need to be feeling words. Your infant may even be connecting words for short sentences. The next aspect of the socialization task that has to do with affective responding is to teach your child how to express emotions verbally. You are the role model; the child will mimic your example. I recommend a simple formula: I feel *angry* when *the dog dirties the rug.*
- Hang pictures around the infant's room that depict an array of emotions, not just those that show happy faces. Talk to your child about the feelings expressed within each picture.

- Ask your child what she feels. Whether you expect her to answer you or not, ask. When the child does answer, give as much attention and respect to her feeling as you would want for your own. You need to practice now what you want your child to play-act when he is three and four years old.

When developing healthy anger, self-possession—the sense that not all I do and am capable of is dependent on the will of others or the whim of the environment—is an important acquisition. It may be helpful to look at figure B in chapter 3 (see page 49). *Self-possession* is one aspect of the Sense of Adequacy a person needs to refrain from overidentifying events as perceived threats, a situation that produces unnecessary anger. Even though infancy is the most vulnerable, dependent time in a human's life, as babies start to move and reach for objects, they can begin reducing the inherent vulnerability of infancy by experiencing self-possession through achieving goals.[7] Here are three ways to assist the child in this endeavor:

- Help her overcome some frustrations and periodically achieve goals. Earlier, when discussing self-regulation and frustration, I recommended that you allow infants time and space to self-soothe or that you provide an object for distraction. Now I would like to add this third option. If your child reaches for her favorite toy, cannot quite get it, and begins to fuss, place it just within reach. This provides a sense of achievement and mastery, two important aspects of self-possession.
- Provide your infant personal autonomy through the game "throw the object off the high chair so the adult has to fetch it." I have not met a baby who did not know this game. The adult places the infant in the high chair, puts down a spoon and a plastic bowl, turns his back to get something, and the youngster flings the spoon or the bowl across the room. The adult puts whatever object went flying back onto the high chair tray. The infant reaches to fling again. You can use a string to tie an object to the high chair. When the baby throws the object, show him how he can use the string to pull the object back. Take time to help him do it. He will learn how very quickly. Not only will this enhance your child's sense of self-possession and emotional glee, it will also help to reduce your frustration level.

- In the last quarter of this developmental phase, your infant probably becomes mobile and begins exploring the immediate environment. Secure a large mirror within her view. Let her see herself and recognize herself as a separate entity from other people and nearby objects. And most important, be there as a place of safety where she can return when the explorations tire or frighten her. The infant who learns to trust her world will develop into a person who rarely misinterprets neutral or benign events as danger-laden, thus reducing inappropriate anger.

Taking Action

Infants depend on sensory stimulation concerning environmental cues. Since babies do not cognitively process information in the same manner as an adult, overstimulation happens on a regular basis. As a caregiver, what are the specific things you will do to help your infant experience emotional safety and trust? Keep in mind the following ideas.

Self-regulation:

Emotional communication:

Overstimulation:

Frustration:

Develop a plan that teaches your infant how to recognize and label feelings. Keep in mind the importance of familiarity with emotions.

Throughout infancy:

First six months:

Six to eighteen months:

Eighteen months plus:

TODDLERS/PRESCHOOLERS (TWO YEARS TO SIX YEARS)

During the toddler/preschool stage of development essential elements within each component of the feeling circle materialize. The elements with the greatest impact on anger involve the origination of self-evaluations in the Thought component, the shaping of socially acceptable expressions of angry feelings in the Behavior component, and the formulation of empathic abilities facilitated by the increased awareness of feeling states in the Emotion component. Parents or other caregivers can facilitate the development of these elements by using specific responses to the youngster's anger. Also, developmentally appropriate activities can assist the child in producing healthy expressions of angry feelings.

The following guidelines will make these activities and exercises easier to implement. Not only do these suggestions have the potential to increase the effectiveness of the activities and exercises in this section, but they also enhance the success of the activities in other sections of this chapter and in the following chapter, "Effectively Responding to Angry Adolescents."

- Speak directly and specifically. There are many behaviors adults take for granted that toddlers and preschoolers have no idea about. How to express anger is one such behavior. Therefore, when the youngster acts out inappropriately, it is not enough to describe how not to act. Children need you to describe specific behaviors that are appropriate. For example, if the child has been shouting, give directions by saying, "Use your indoor voice." It might help to demonstrate how that sounds. As the child grows older, more sophisticated language is appropriate.

• Provide consistency. Children learn fastest when confusion is reduced through consistency. Let the young person know what behaviors are acceptable and then direct the child on those behaviors before he loses control. Maintain the same expectations and respond each time using similar response styles. Consistency requires that, as role models, primary caregivers express their anger in the same or similar manner they expect from the child.

• Show respect. Often I have to remind myself that all things are relative. The toddler is probably angry because of some frustration. The preschooler toward the end stages of this developmental period may be angry because of an interpersonal reaction. Their frustration or situation may seem small to us, but we are big. The problem seems big to them because they are small, with many limitations. The very least adults can do is to show respect concerning the distress the child is experiencing by listening and exercising politeness.

• Focus on the positive as much as possible. Some children act out to get attention. If you point out what they are doing wrong constantly, they learn to engage you by doing wrong. Notice in the example I used above to illustrate how to speak directly and specifically, I did not recommend that you tell the child to stop shouting. Instead, I suggested that you focus on the positive behavioral outcome you want— a quieter tone of voice. There is one exception to this guideline. Any physical aggression by the child needs to be responded to by informing the youngster that the behavior is not acceptable.

• Pick your battles. Limit the number of rules and expectations you thrust upon the young person. The more you have, the more you have to enforce. The more you enforce, the greater chances there are for frustrations and power struggles with your child.

The *origination of self-evaluations* usually begins around age three, when a child becomes conscious of a personal existence and various relationships to others in the immediate environment.[8] The original self-evaluations are so crucial to developing a child's self-esteem, and hence the interpretation of events, that it is important to ensure the number of positive messages the youngster internalizes exceeds the amount of negative ones.

Keeping a healthy balance regarding feedback is difficult because preschoolers tend to internalize criticism as a judgment of themselves as people rather than a commentary on one specific behavior. Most child care specialists now agree that caregivers need to separate what the child does from his value as a person by clearly directing any criticism at the behavior. Unfortunately, because children in this age group are so sensitive to and involved in developing who they are in relationship to their environment, just redirecting criticism is not enough. Even with behaviorally directed feedback, a child may still internalize critiques as a judgment of self and form a negative self-evaluation from those critiques. The negative message must be interrupted before it becomes an intrinsic part of the child's self-esteem.

In responding to a preschooler's anger, the problem of internalization of negative self-evaluations usually occurs when the youngster has expressed angry feelings in a destructive or hurtful way. The guiding tenet in this situation is to condemn the behavior while appreciating the child. The basic formula a friend of mine uses is: "I want to be really clear. Even though I don't like how you were acting, I still love you." The one that suits me is: "Even though I don't like that you *threw your truck,* you are *still an important member of this family.* Will you help me with *dinner?*" The words you choose may change with each new incident, but the general meaning and structure of the response remains. It includes the unacceptable behavior and then a positive message that appreciates the child.

In chapter 4, I listed a number of common negative self-evaluations that result in a denying self-concept. To develop an affirming self-concept, it is important to circumvent the internalization of negative evaluations by stating the opposite, positive evaluations. Then ask the child to help you. At this age, children like to help adults. Also, helping actively affirms the positive statement. Someone who helps is important, is worthwhile, is good enough. If you are not about to do anything that the child can help with, think of some other activity that you and the child can do together.

Encouraging Positive Self-Evaluations

You will have a better chance of responding effectively to your child's anger if you have clear ideas formed about what you want to say and how you want to say it. You will be even more effective if you mentally practice your responses before an incident occurs. The following exercise will help you with this process. Think of three times when your child has aggressively acted out, and then fill in your ideas.

Incident #1:

Condemn the behavior:

Appreciate the child:

Suggest an activity:

Incident #2:

Condemn the behavior:

Appreciate the child:

Suggest an activity:

Incident #3:

Condemn the behavior:

Appreciate the child:

Suggest an activity:

As you do your daily relaxation session, when you have become re-laxed, visualize the first incident. As you replay it mentally, substitute what actually happened with your new examples that condemn the behavior, ap-preciate the child, and suggest an activity. Do the same for the other two in-cidents. Practice in this manner until your child acts out and you use your new method of responding.

The construction of an affirming self-concept involves the child's capac-ity to think of herself as an individual entity and to evaluate that entity in relationship to other separate entities. Once the youngster recognizes that there is a me and there is a you, the *formulation of empathic abilities* begins to emerge.[9] This is another uniquely human characteristic with the potential to significantly modify aggressive, even fatally violent, behavior. One after-noon a Vietnam veteran told me about the experience that interrupted his career as a soldier. He said, "I had him [the enemy] in my sights, ready to fire, when I thought, 'I wonder if he misses his family too?' And I couldn't pull the trigger."

Empathy consists of two separate internal activities. One is based in the Thought component of the feeling circle and the other activity is present in the Emotion component. The thought aspect of empathy involves assuming the perspective of another person, putting oneself in another's position, and looking at events from that new angle.

There are a number of ways to help your preschooler practice taking different perspectives.[10] These include:

- When you watch videos or TV programs with your youngster, ask him what he thinks various characters are thinking. *The Wizard of Oz* and *Stuart Little* are excellent movies to use in this activity.
- If you have a pet, ask your child what she would see if she were in its place.
- Ask, "What do you think that bird sees when it flies over our house, or that butterfly as it sits on a flower, or that squirrel when it runs across the telephone wire?"
- If your preschooler brings home a tale about something that happened at day care or the babysitter's, ask him what each person involved might have been thinking.

There are two skills a person must have to experience and share the aspect of empathy that resides in the Emotion component. The individual must be able to imagine the feeling state of another person and, while experiencing the imagined emotion, must be able to name it with a label recognizable by others. Children in this age range have acquired the ability to experience and name guilt, as well as mad, glad, sad, and afraid. There are a number of ways to help the preschooler imagine another person's emotional state and label these feelings.

- While watching a movie or a TV program, ask your child what the various characters are feeling during different scenes. Again, *The Wizard of Oz* is excellent for this activity. The entire range of human emotions is present and the characters' faces and gestures clearly demonstrate the characters' feelings. If your child is not able to label the emotions, help by making statements like, "Gee, if that were me, I'd feel (give a feeling label)."
- Look through magazines with your preschooler. Stop at pictures with people. Help each other decide what the people are feeling and what you might feel in their places.

Practicing Different Perspectives

How will you help your preschooler learn to take different perspectives? You can use some of the activities I have listed, and you can create your own. Write out a week's plan of activities. Use specifics. If you are going to watch a movie, give the name of the movie and the time. You do not have to fill in all blank spaces, and you can have additional activities beyond the number of blank spaces provided.

Monday
Activity _____ Time _____
Activity _____ Time _____
Activity _____ Time _____

Tuesday
Activity _____ Time _____
Activity _____ Time _____
Activity _____ Time _____

Wednesday
Activity _____ Time _____
Activity _____ Time _____
Activity _____ Time _____

Thursday
Activity _____ Time _____
Activity _____ Time _____
Activity _____ Time _____

Friday
Activity _____ Time _____
Activity _____ Time _____
Activity _____ Time _____

Saturday
Activity ——————————— Time —————————————
Activity ——————————— Time —————————————
Activity ——————————— Time —————————————
Activity ——————————— Time —————————————
Activity ——————————— Time —————————————

Sunday
Activity ——————————— Time —————————————
Activity ——————————— Time —————————————
Activity ——————————— Time —————————————
Activity ——————————— Time —————————————
Activity ——————————— Time —————————————

Understanding Each Feeling's Purpose

As a youngster nears age five or six, elementary school is imminent. Before your child enters this more intensified social environment, learning the function of each emotion can be beneficial. It is helpful to keep explanations simple and concrete. With that edict in mind, determine each emotion's purpose. (Chapter 2 lists a number of ideas concerning the functionality of each feeling.) Then remember a time your child, a friend, a favorite fictional character, or family member used it for that purpose. In preparation for this, complete the following.

Anger's purpose(s):

The incident when used:

Sadness's purpose(s):

The incident when used:

1

Guilt's purpose(s):

The incident when used:

Fear's purpose(s):

The incident when used:

Happiness's purpose(s):

The incident when used:

The next time you and your child are looking at a magazine or reading a story and you talk about the character's feelings, add the above information to the discussion.

If your child is able to respond empathetically to others, any tendencies toward aggression will be minimized, lessening the efforts needed to teach socially acceptable, nonaggressive behaviors. Most parents that I have counseled focus their attention on the Behavior component of the feeling circle to the exclusion of the other components. They want to know how to change their child's expressions of anger. Because of the circular nature of the emotion process, it is possible, if consistency is maintained, to effect lasting change by aiming your reaction at only the Behavior area. My response to parents who are concerned only with their child's conduct: Shaping socially acceptable behaviors that express angry feelings requires you to

- respond positively to the acceptable
- intervene on the dangerous
- ignore the unpleasant

When helping the toddler or preschooler learn how to express anger in an acceptable manner, the first task is to decide what behaviors belong in which of the three categories. Remember, when you go about making this determination, you need to be prepared to practice the ones you deem acceptable and forego those that are dangerous or unpleasant. You are the role model, the agent of socialization for your children, and beginning around age three, children begin to mimic almost everything they see adults doing or saying.

Determining Acceptable Behaviors

I believe that *almost* any verbalization by the child can be fashioned into an acceptable behavior if you do not interpret the angry words as an indictment of your parenting abilities, overreacting to what was said or how it was said. Also, I am aware that families from different cultures judge children's behaviors differently. Therefore, from the list below, decide which behaviors that you would place in the given categories by marking *acceptable, dangerous,* or *obnoxious* next to the corresponding behavior. There may be some behaviors that I have not specified that you are concerned get placed in a certain category. Please add them in the blank spaces provided at the end of the list.

_____ "no" in a firm tone		_____ "I'm mad"
_____ hitting		_____ ignoring you
_____ yelling		_____ "I don't like this"
_____ name-calling		_____ biting
_____ "I don't want_____"		_____ a defiant response
_____ kicking		_____ "I hate you"
_____ pouting		_____ profanity
_____ "I want_____"		_____ "I'm angry"
_____ throwing/breaking objects		_____ pinching
_____		_____
_____		_____

When your child demonstrates a behavior you deemed acceptable, your positive response encourages a similar expression of angry feelings in the future. Praising and rewarding a behavior, however, is not a positive way of responding, no matter how wonderful that behavior was. Instead, a positive response style involves validation, attention, and interaction.

The first step is to validate the feeling by responding in one of the following ways:

- What are you angry about?
- I can see you are angry. What is that about?

Next, be attentive by listening carefully and nondefensively. This means that you look at your child as he speaks to you. Kneel down so that you are on an equal level with each other. Ask for clarification if you do not understand what your child is saying.

Depending upon the information presented, you may need to engage your child through discussion or negotiation. Above all else, when you make a mistake, own up to it. "Gee, you've got a point. What can we do to fix this?" is a response that, in the long term, will provide your child with a number of benefits. With it, you teach that there is no shame in making a mistake, you demonstrate how to react when a mistake is brought up, and you model the idea of looking for solutions instead of belaboring the problem.

Behaviors that you indicated as dangerous, meaning physically harmful to your child or others, must be addressed actively and immediately. Hitting and biting mean that your youngster has lost control.[11] This can be very frightening for your child. Therefore, it is important that you remain calm (use the quick calming technique practiced in chapter 5), physically stop the harmful behavior, and state, "You may not . . . That is not acceptable behavior." Hold your child or take him to a place where you can sit together until he calms down enough for you to discuss what happened. When you find out what triggered the aggression, validate the anger and suggest an alternative way of handling it. Examples of how this is done are the following:

- "It's okay that you feel angry. The next time you feel that way, show it by . . . or by . . ."
- "I understand you felt angry about that. A good way to show you're mad is to . . ."

Teaching Anger Responses

Now is the time to determine how you want your child to express anger. Earlier you indicated acceptable expressions. At this point you have the opportunity to teach the preferable. During this developmental period children go from frustration-triggered anger to object anger (conflict over possession). Some children may even experience interpersonal anger (conflict resulting from personal interactions such as threats or status). Each of these categories of anger provocation can be resolved through different approaches. Frustration caused by the inability to attain a desired goal might best be addressed through problem solving. Object use might call for negotiation, while personal interactions might require empathy or discussion. Describe how you would prefer the child to express anger triggered by

Frustration:

Object use or possession:

Personal interactions:

What sentences are you comfortable saying to validate anger? Think of three so that you have options.

Anger validation:

Anger validation:

Anger validation:

Put a validation sentence and the preferable anger response together for anger triggered by

Frustration:

Object use or possession:

Personal interaction:

Do not hit or bite or pinch toddlers and preschoolers to show what the hurtful action feels like. By doing so you are modeling aggressive, violent behaviors, and your child will probably follow your example by continuing to act out in a similar fashion.

I am convinced that there are two times in a young person's life that are especially hard on the parents: "the terrible twos" and the "terrible teens." Both of these time frames are typified by new autonomy, limited skill, and power struggles. How these variables manifest during the teen years is discussed in the next chapter. For toddlers and preschoolers, their manifestations occur in irritatingly expressed frustration and anger. This is the common developmental stage for temper tantrums, passive and active defiance, and a host of other obnoxious behaviors. The most productive response consists of the following process:[12]

- Remain calm while you make sure that your child is safe and not going to incur harm.
- Then ignore the behavior. Without any type of reinforcement, the an-

noying, irritating acting out will extinguish. For this to happen, you must be consistent by ignoring the behavior every time your preschooler does it.

- Once the obnoxious behavior has subsided, respond in a nurturing way. Let the child know that you still love her and that she is still important to you. I recently recommended this to a parent, and her response was, "I am not going to reward a temper tantrum by hugging him." A parent's love is not a child's reward, it is her birthright. A child who has had a temper tantrum has lost control, creating a great deal of fear. She needs comforting, and she needs to know that she is still loved.

- Since temper tantrums are usually triggered by frustration, suggest acceptable, constructive ways that frustration can be handled.

Children beginning this phase of development experience anger and act out aggressively because of frustration. They are separating from their mothers and gaining a new independence. They want to experiment and try new things. But their ability to perform is limited, and they cannot do the new things they try. They become frustrated and angry. As they move toward the end of the preschool phase, their anger becomes more object oriented. Someone takes away an object and anger ensues. Even with these differences, all of the suggestions presented in this section will provide positive results throughout this age group. In fact, with some modifications to make them age appropriate, these responses to anger can be effective with children of the next developmental phase.

SCHOOL-AGED CHILDREN (SIX YEARS TO TEN YEARS)

Ask a five- or six-year-old how to handle anger, and he will suggest a way to manipulate the situation to his liking. Ask the same question of a ten-year-old, and she might explain how she will adjust her thoughts. The shift from blaming anger on external obstacles to recognizing the influence of thought on the internal emotional reaction is one area of developmental growth that occurs during these four years. Other changes also affect anger during this age period:

- Cooperative play replaces associative play.[13]

- Display rules are learned and implemented.
- Aggressive behavior is not tolerated as easily by peers.[14]
- Self-esteem displaces objects as the major focus of anger.

These four years, the first years of formal schooling, are the child's initial experience with socialization by peer interaction. Even if a child attended day care or preschool, the experience produced minimal socialization by peers in comparison to what happens in elementary school. The associative play of preschool children requires only a modicum of interchange between schoolmates. Around the age of seven, however, children begin to play cooperatively. This type of play, consisting of a mutually developed goal or theme, rules, resolution of conflict, and role exchanges, requires the child to be accepted by other students. This need for acceptance, with its reward of being included in play, is a strong incentive to change behavior in order to fit in. Parents or other significant adults of children in elementary school can have an impact on their efforts at peer acceptance. Children whose parents are expressive with their feelings exhibit the least aggression and the most emotional expression, while being the most popular among their peers.[15]

Even after hearing me make that statement, parents frequently ask me if they should show anger toward each other in front of their children. My answer is a strong yes, with these two conditions:

1. Review chapter 7 and use the safety guidelines that you developed there.
2. Resolve the anger openly. Any harm that might have resulted from the tension of the conflict will be mitigated when the child witnesses the resolution.[16]

Part of peer inclusion during this initial socially interactive phase of development requires children to grasp and implement display rules. Display rules are social guidelines for controlling and expressing emotions. Children learn what feelings are acceptable to express and how to express them in a manner deemed socially appropriate. Also, as the flip side of this process, the school-aged child ascertains which feelings are not acceptable and, therefore, need to be hidden from public view, either through the use of defense mechanisms or by the replacement of one emotion with another that carries greater social approval. In the United States, boys experiencing this socialization process tend to hide fear and sadness, and girls tend to conceal anger.[17]

Understanding the rules that dictate social appropriateness for the expression of feelings is helpful to youngsters because they are required to behave within acceptable parameters. But when the rules are internalized and practiced to the extent that certain basic emotions are denied continuously, the child loses the ability to recognize and label those internal feeling sensations. When a school-aged boy experiences this phenomenon, he tends to substitute anger for fear and sadness.[18] By doing this, he appears to possess an overly abundant amount of anger that sometimes seems incongruent with the instigating event. A school-aged girl, on the other hand, tends to defensively hide angry feelings. In doing so, she loses the ability to access the many functions of anger.

Parents can help their child avoid these socially induced emotional traps by expressing these three troublesome feelings when they occur and by sharing personal stories about experiences that generated one or more of these feelings.

Below, list three incidents when you have been afraid that you can share with your child. Try to recount at least one incident from a time during your youth.

I felt afraid when

I felt afraid when

I felt afraid when

Now, do the same by listing times when you have felt sad.

I felt sad when

I felt sad when

I felt sad when

Do the same as above, using the feeling of anger.

I felt angry when

I felt angry when

I felt angry when

Children of this age group enjoy stories. Every so often, forego a half-hour of television and, while you are saying goodnight to your child, share one of the incidents above as a story. When you finish, ask your child if there is a time when he had a similar feeling. Discuss the incident and the emotion in an affirming way.

A meaningful technique that can help children throughout their lives involves teaching them how to evaluate events to determine what motivated the people involved. Did someone intend to be hostile or was something else going on? Researchers studying children in classrooms are finding that most reactive aggression is the result of one child attributing hostility to another child's behavior when no hostility was intended.[19] In other words, the majority of children who use aggression to react to other people often are misinterpreting the event. When you respond to this particular problem, it is important that you help your child realize that behavior can be motivated by reasons other than hostility or hurtful intentions. There are two easy ways to do this. Which one you use depends upon the target of the child's anger.

If your child is angry toward you, there are a number of questions you can ask to see how the youngster is interpreting your motives:

- What did you think I was going to do?
- How did you think I would react?
- Why do you think I did (or said) that?

Then, discuss the child's answer. Maybe she thought you were going to hit her. Maybe he thought a decision you made was unfair. Or maybe she decided you did it because you do not like her. Listen to the answer carefully and then respond in a nondefensive manner using this formula:

I feel ＿＿＿＿＿＿＿＿＿＿ when ＿＿＿＿＿＿＿＿＿＿ .

For example, if a young person told me that she thought I would spank her, I would probably say: "I feel sad hearing that. I can't imagine hurting you that way. It's okay that you feel angry. I hope next time you will ask me."

If the child's anger is directed at a third person, I recommend that, after the youngster is controlled, you ask: "Why do you think he (or she) did (or said) that?"

Next, guide the child toward finding at least two other (nonhostile) reasons that might explain the other person's behavior. With children this young, ask about reasons one at a time. If you have witnessed a child's aggression, think of potential answers to these questions.

What's another reason he might have done that?
Answer: ＿＿＿＿＿＿＿＿＿＿＿＿＿＿ .

And what's another reason he might have done that?

Answer: _____ .

    Finally, help your child understand that it is okay to feel angry and that sometimes anger is generated by how we look at a situation rather than what actually happened. Then work with the youngster to ask questions concerning the person's motive.

    As a means of reinforcing the idea that there are multiple reasons possible for a person's behavior, you can encourage the child to think about the intent behind other people's actions. It is difficult to help a person learn how to think, because cognitive activity occurs within the mind, making it invisible. But to assist a child who responds to benign or neutral events as though they are hostile, it is important that you make the effort. To succeed, you are going to make the internal phenomenon of thinking into an external activity by modeling self-talk. This procedure is very similar to the self-talk exercise that you practiced in chapter 5. Instead of thinking the self-talk silently, when an anger-arousing situation happens, talk out loud so your child can hear it. Pick words that you know your child understands, and apply them to the following process.

- Stop. I need to stop for a minute.
- Take a deep breath and relax.
- I'm feeling angry. Jan is twenty minutes late.
- I bet she's doing this to get even. Maybe not. I'll ask her when she arrives [clarification of motive]. Maybe she couldn't help being late.

    The self-talk above can help the child understand that there may be more than one possible motive for another person's behavior, and that before reacting to a potentially misread event, you can investigate for intent by asking questions.

    Along with the expectation of belligerent or hostile motives from others, there are any number of reasons that a school-aged child experiences anger. Frustrating obstacles, conflict over object possession, negative temperament, or vying for the adult's time is a short list of those reasons. As the child's anger focus expands out from objects to include self-esteem, the need to protect against put-downs, teasing, and public humiliation increases the list.

    Asking questions to clarify an event helps the child understand its nature, making it more likely the child will choose a constructive behavioral response. Three proactive behaviors can be easily taught to children in this age group: negotiation, assertiveness, and assistance. Before explicitly practicing these three skills with your child, you can begin teaching them by adding these alternatives into the self-talk process. It will then look like this:

- Stop. I need to stop for a minute.
- Take a deep breath and relax.
- I'm feeling angry. Jan is twenty minutes late.
- I bet she's doing this to get even. Maybe not. I'll ask her when she arrives [clarification of motive]. Maybe she couldn't help being late. Even if she couldn't help it, maybe we can work something out where she will call me next time [negotiation strategy].
- If she did do it on purpose, then I'll decide if I need my anger to stand up for myself. I'll let her know how I feel and what I need from her [assertiveness strategy].
- Or maybe she will listen to her father more than me. I could ask him to help me talk with her [assistance strategy].

Since you are saying this in front of the child, you may want to ask which of the two end alternatives he would choose and why.

Please note how the last option, seeking assistance, was worded. Rather than, "I'll ask him to talk with her," it says, "I'll ask him to help me talk with her." I do not recommend that you give the child the idea that another person is going to "fix" the situation. The message to send is this: Each person has anger, each is responsible for its use. That does not mean that a person cannot ask for help when implementing an assertiveness strategy. In fact, there are many instances when assistance is advisable, especially in elementary school, where there is the potential for bullying.

Before trying the self-talk out on your child, you might want to practice. Think of a time when you were angry with someone and you could have used a negotiation strategy to resolve the problem. Write down how you could have self-talked that in front of your child.

- Stop. I need to stop for a minute.
- Take a deep breath and relax.
- I feel angry that:

- Clarification of motive:
- Negotiation strategy:

Now say the entire exercise out loud, as though your child were present.
Think of another time when you were angry with someone and could have used assertiveness to meet your needs. Write down how you could have self-talked that in front of your child.

- Stop. I need to stop for a minute.
- Take a deep breath and relax.
- I feel angry that:
- Clarification of motive:
- Assertiveness statement:

Again, say the entire exercise out loud, as though your child were present.
Think of another time when you were angry with someone and you could have sought help to resolve the problem. Write down how you could have self-talked that in front of your child.

- Stop. I need to stop for a minute.
- Take a deep breath and relax.
- I feel angry that:
- Clarification of motive:
- Possible assistance:

Again, say the entire exercise out loud, as though your child were present.
The above exercise is designed to help children process their thoughts and strategize on how to use anger. When a youngster is angry with you or with another child, use these same methods to respond. Would the situation best be handled by saying, "I can see you're angry. Perhaps there is a way we can work this out so we both get what we want," or "You look angry. What do you need?"

If you need to respond to a conflict over possession of an object, assist the children in learning how to negotiate for time with the object. Remember that the younger children of this age group have no concept of time length. The suggestion that each child have the object for ten minutes is not going to be helpful. A minute, or ten minutes, or an hour has limited if any meaning for them. You will need to pick a concrete measure of time such as setting a timer with a bell or the end of a television show.

Knowing When to Use What

There are three basic behavioral response styles children of this age group can use to express and respond to anger constructively: negotiation, assertiveness, and assistance. It is important that they know which to use in a given situation, as well as how to use it. By completing this exercise, you will have clear ideas on how and when you want each response style implemented. When the next inappropriate expression of anger occurs, you will be prepared to direct your child in using these response styles. Below are the three basic styles. List situations from the past in which your child could have used each intervention. Then provide a general formula for how you would have the child implement the intervention.

Assertiveness

Previous situation:

Previous situation:

Basic formula:

Negotiation

Previous situation:

Previous situation:

Basic formula:

Seeking Assistance

Previous situation:

Previous situation:

Basic formula:

When you intervene on an aggressive act, such as hitting, either because you see the violence or because one of the children solicits your help, state clearly to the offender, "Hitting hurts. It is not allowed here." Then request the offended youth to state what he wants and to express how he feels about being hit. Also, it is important to present alternative behaviors for the hitter to choose from. Perhaps he was provoked by the first child and needs to learn how to be assertive instead of aggressive. Help him decide on a feeling statement concerning his emotional response to the provocation (I felt angry). Investigate what he would like the other child to do instead of the provocative behavior (Leave me alone). Inquire if the child thinks he can say that next time. If he says yes, ask, "Will you let me hear you say it now?" After he says it, reinforce that with a compliment on how well he did it. Then ask, "Can I hear you say it one more time?" The more he repeats the statement, the more likely he is to use it when provoked.

Anger is a form of communication. When angry, whether expressed with words or physical aggression, the youngster is trying to convey a message. Preferably, language will be the medium chosen for the communiqué. If the child has a violent episode, the first goal is to help the young person regain personal control. Once this is accomplished, the following process presents a method for teaching an assertive response style.

- Help the child grasp an understanding of the specific message that was behind the acting-out behavior. Talk with the child to review the events that led up to the aggression. This often provides insight into the behavior's meaning.
- Once you think you know what precipitated the aggressive action, verify your guess with the child. When both of you have an accurate understanding of the event that triggered the behavior and the intended message that it conveyed, help the youngster connect the message with an anger statement.
- Ask the youngster to repeat the assertive statement that you just created. Verbal repetition acts to solidify the acceptable form of communication into the child's cache of behavioral alternatives, making it more probable the child will choose that alternative the next time a similar situation arises.

PREADOLESCENCE (TEN YEARS TO FOURTEEN YEARS)

Recently, a teacher asked a thirteen-year-old boy to leave school on the last day of class because he had been throwing water balloons. The boy went home and later returned to ask his teacher for readmission. He wanted to see two girls in the class, one of whom was his girlfriend. When the request was denied, the thirteen-year-old pointed his grandfather's gun at the teacher and fatally shot him in the head. The boy's lawyer, while arguing that his client not be tried as an adult, discussed how he thought that Nathaniel understood the charges against him, but he didn't believe the boy had contemplated the prospect of life in prison without parole until he dies.[20] This assessment is probably accurate. For a child in this age range, the immediacy of the emotional consequences of losing face or failing a school year takes precedence over the possible long-term consequences imposed by the criminal justice system.

The boy's solitary and impulsive act of violence ended his teacher's life and drastically modified his own forever. Although this is an extreme case of violence, the isolative and impulsive nature with which it was done is typical for aggressive children of this age group. Nathaniel was an intelligent youngster who liked school and the teacher he shot. If he had slowed down to weigh the results of his actions, would he have carried out the murder? Probably not. Research studies of aggressive behaviors by youngsters at this age indicate that quick interpretation of the event and fast follow-through result in more physical, instead of verbal, reactions.[21]

Therefore, the most beneficial approach for you to use with your pre-adolescent involves teaching deliberate assessment of the event and productive uses of the energy that accompanies anger. This is accomplished by helping your child understand the four-step method for using anger. There are two possible ways to do this. The first way is used when your child is expressing anger about a situation that does not involve you. This presents a perfect opportunity to describe how to use anger as a way to make changes. To do this, explain the following:

1. It is okay to feel angry, and that anger is a good motivator for change.
2. It is important to take a deep breath and slow down so that the exact pieces of the situation creating the anger can be recognized or, if necessary, changed.
3. A vast number of different actions will modify the situation. Decide on the best way the situation could be changed without hurting yourself or others.
4. While still energized by the anger, think of and take the first step necessary to initiate the change.

Presenting this method of how to use anger will be more meaningful to your child if you can give an example of how it has worked for you. If you were to do that, it might sound something like this:

1. Remember when you were seven or eight and I would get so angry with your aunt Jan. She was always late, and I relied on her to drive me to work.
2. Finally I took a deep breath, stood back, and really thought about it. Not only did her being late waste my time, it also gave her control over a piece of my life.
3. I talked with her, and she agreed to call whenever she was going to be late. But she still had piece of control over my life, and I didn't like

that. I decided that I was angry enough to go without some things if it allowed me to save money every week.

4. That week I found a way to save fifty dollars. After two years I had enough money to buy that old car. It may be old and it may guzzle gas. But it gives me back control of when I go and when I stay.

Presenting the Four-Step Process

Think of a situation when you were angry and either used, or could have used, the four-step process. Then complete the steps below.

1. You felt angry. Incident:

2. Take a deep breath to slow down. What parts of the situation were you angry about?

3. What were some potential ways to change those pieces of the situation that you feel angry about?

Which one of these offered the greatest benefit without being destructive to you or someone else?

4. What is one thing you could have done, while still angry, to initiate the plan to make this change?

The second method of helping your child learn this process is to externalize it as self-talk, using the same method described in the previous section on school-aged children. Remember to slow yourself down with deep breaths and talk your way through the steps so your child can hear and understand each step. On step three, you may want to:

- State one or two changes and then ask if your child can think of any to add.
- Ask, with each idea for change on the list, "Who might be harmed by that?"
- Include your child in choosing the best plan for change. Once you make a choice, say something such as, "Let's make sure we can't think of anyone who will be hurt by that."

There are going to be times when you do not have the time or energy to self-talk the entire process involved in the productive use of anger. There are two extremely important points in the process that interrupt a preadolescent's tendency to act in an impulsive, hurtful way: slowing down to assess the situation and evaluating potential harm to self and others. Because of this, you can implement the desired interruption by verbalizing either of these process pieces. If you choose this method, it might sound like this:

- "Boy, that ticks me off. I need to take a deep breath, slow down, and think of what I'm really angry about here."
- State an idea for change and then add, "I wonder who might get hurt if I do that."
- "I'd like to punch his lights out. Wait! How will that hurt him and me?"

Preadolescents are moving away from childhood and toward adolescence. They see older siblings or neighbors with more freedom and greater personal power. Those privileges appear enticing, and so these children ask for similar power and freedom. When you as the parent, knowing the preadolescent is still too immature to handle as much responsibility as the older sibling or neighbor, responds with a firm no, a belligerent conflict erupts. It is up to you, as the adult, to get the flare-up under control. One effective way to do this is to use the two-part statement: "I really do want to understand what you are saying. If we both take a breath and slow down, I think I can listen better."

Then as you listen, ask yourself if there is any way to negotiate a compromise. If safety is not a concern and you think the situation is negotiable, respond to your child with, "I am willing to negotiate a compromise. Are you?" If your child is not, stick to your initial response and explain why you decided that way. If your child is ready to compromise, ask your child to make an offer. When the offer is made and you still hesitate, make a counteroffer. Continue the negotiations until you arrive at the point where you are no longer willing to give more. The youngster then has the choice of taking the compromise or not. Your child has the personal power of choice.

Knowing What Is Negotiable

In order to negotiate effectively as a parent, you need to be aware of the situations about which you are not willing to negotiate. Make a list of those situations and keep them in mind when your child asks for permission to try something new.

I will not negotiate:

Preadolescents have what seems to be a deep need to mask any appearance of wrongdoing. This, in and of itself, is not especially annoying. The irritation occurs in the way that the young person attempts to avoid the responsibility. Usually the method of choice is defensively, and at times sarcastically, refocusing the discussion by accusing the adult of a similar misdeed. For example, I have a colleague who is convinced that the fashion designers of the world were out to get her when they hit on the fad of baggy clothes. This one particular social phenomenon created a vast amount of problems in my co-worker's life because it meant that her clothes were no longer too big for her thirteen-year-old daughter. One cool fall evening she went to get her favorite sweatshirt and could not find it. She asked her daughter if she knew what happened to it. The girl explained that she had taken it to the beach and somehow lost it. Angry, my co-worker exclaimed, "You lost my favorite sweatshirt!"

In a voice that my colleague described as dripping with hostility, her daughter responded, "Well, I suppose you never borrowed something and lost it."

My co-worker took a breath, gathered her thoughts, and said, "Right now that's not the point. You lost my sweatshirt. That means I am without a sweatshirt and I'm angry. How are you going to pay me for it?" She worked out a deal with her daughter that involved housework as compensation for the lost sweatshirt.

One possible explanation for why preadolescents are so sensitive about mistakes and why they tend to deal with that sensitivity by angrily accusing adults of similar offenses is that they are beginning to realize that the parents they depended on as a godlike figures have turned out to be imperfect and vulnerable. Recognition of this fact makes the child's world less safe. When safety is compromised, anger emerges as a protective shield.

Adults need to help children develop the ability to experience, rather than deny, their humanity. Human beings make mistakes. This is reality. Adults can assist children in coming to accept this reality, while responding effectively to the anger, by confirming their own mistakes without overreacting to the accusation. I witnessed a father, a recovering addict, employ this response mechanism when he confronted his twelve-year-old son about smoking marijuana. His son responded with hostility, "Who are you to talk? You can't tell me you haven't smoked weed!"

The father answered, "You're right. I made that mistake. It's why I get so afraid when I think you're making the same one. And that's why I want to discuss your marijuana use now."

This father did not hide his mistake; he shared a feeling and refocused the attention back onto the child's behavior. If the situation being addressed is not as serious as potential drug abuse, you can add an invitation to discuss your mistake at a later time.

Holding the Focus Where It Belongs

If your child tends to use this particular defensive maneuver, you might want to think about the separate pieces of the suggested response. Remember a confrontation when your child turned the tables and accused you of a similar mistake or misbehavior.

What was the confrontation?

How did your child accuse you?

How could you have confirmed the mistake?

How could you have shared your feeling and refocused the attention back onto your child's behavior?

If it would have been appropriate to discuss your mistake at a later time, how could you have indicated that?

I began this section by presenting a specific incident of violence, the killing of a Florida teacher by a student. This event was on CNN's national news and on the CBS news, as headlined by America Online. As I watched and later read the news, I imagined that it sent at least a fleeting moment of fear through parents of children that age. I wondered what teachers in other middle schools were thinking as they viewed or read this latest tragedy happening within a work environment similar to their own.

Is all of the fear generated by this type of hype valid? Are middle schools dangerous places for our children? What can parents do to provide greater safety for their children? To help put all of this in perspective, I have listed below some research findings concerning the violence of fighting and weapon carrying by youth aged ten to fourteen.

- About 35 percent of the students surveyed in two separate studies

admitted that they had fought while at school the previous year. This
percentage increases with age.[22]

- Students who use mood-altering substances frequently are most likely
  to carry weapons to school.[23]
- Students with parents who used nonviolent discipline fought significantly less than those who had parents who used a form of hitting as
  punishment.[24]
- Fighting was significantly greater for students who thought their parents want them to fight if insulted. Forty-four percent of the students
  surveyed could not remember discussing fighting with parents and
  were deducing their parents' thoughts about fighting.[25]
- Students who try to stay out of fights usually succeed.[26]
- Students who frequently fight are more likely to carry weapons than
  those who do not fight as often.[27]
- Children who spend more time each day watching TV report greater
  levels of violence.[28]
- Children who prefer action/fighting programs had higher levels of
  violent behaviors than children who prefer other types of programming, such as situation comedies.[29]

From the list above, it is possible to extrapolate some simple and effective actions that you, as a parent, can take to minimize the potential involvement of your child in violent acts. Only one of these suggestions costs
money. The rest require your time.

Discipline your child using means other than physical force or hitting.
I recommend the approach that my co-worker took with her daughter who
lost the sweatshirt. How can you pay me for it? Then settle on a payment
that is not too taxing to the young person. In this age range, the idea is to
help the youngster recognize that her behavior affects other people either fi-
nancially or emotionally. To make the situation right requires reimbursing
financial losses and making efforts to repair hurt feelings. If the child and
you cannot think of a way to remedy harm done to someone's emotions,
ask the harmed person. This is an example of disciplining through natural
and logical consequences. (For more on this idea, see pages 238–240.)

Disciplining Natural and Logical Consequences

Think of three times in the past month when you disciplined your child. What discipline did you use? If the discipline did not involve natural and logical consequences, how could they have been employed? Remember to keep the consequences appropriate for the age of your child.

1. What was the misdeed?

Who or what was damaged?

What repair or repayment could have been made?

2. What was the misdeed?

Who or what was damaged?

What repair or repayment could have been made?

3. What was the misdeed?

Who or what was damaged?

What repair or repayment could have been made?

Discuss, using specifics, your beliefs about fighting, violence, and hurting other people. I do not remember ever wanting to perform or defer a performance of any particular deed because it was the nice thing to do or because nice girls don't do it. I do remember being willing to refrain from kicking the little boy next door when my mother explained that it would hurt him. That explanation had meaning for me. I had experienced physical pain and I knew what that felt like. Talking to your children about your beliefs concerning the treatment of others can have a profound and lasting effect on how your youngster expresses personal anger and responds to other people's anger. Therefore, be clear on your beliefs about fighting and other forms of violence. Is it all right to hit someone back? Is it permissible to hit a person who has been insulting? What about hitting someone who has stolen an object from you? When do you fight and when do you walk away?

Clarifying Your Beliefs

Have you spoken with your child about your attitudes and beliefs concerning violent behaviors? Parental attitudes have a powerful influence on a youngster's decision to participate in violence. The questions below will help you clarify some of your beliefs.

What would you have your child do if he or she is

Hit:

Insulted:

A victim of theft:

Subjected to an insult about a family member:

Pushed:

Verbally threatened:

Attacked by one person:

Attacked by a group:

Accused of stealing:

Continually pushed around:

Witness to an attack on another person:

When should your child

Have access to a gun:

Carry a weapon:

Use a gun or other weapon:

If you suspect substance abuse, even substance use, bring your child to a substance abuse professional for an assessment. Almost all parents of teenagers who abuse drugs or alcohol began suspecting that their children were abusing substances twelve to thirty-six months *after* serious drug and/or alcohol use had become part of their child's life. In addition, the teenagers were using at least four times the amount of drugs suspected by the parent. If your child has suddenly had a negative change in attitude, friends, dress, school performance, and behavior (especially aggressive behavior) consider the possibility of substance use. There is no harm in talking with a substance abuse professional. By doing so you may avoid, and help your child avoid, a number of painful consequences.

Pick at least one TV program each night that you will watch together with your entire family and discuss. By doing this, you may negate two potential problems—the negative effects of exposure to television violence and the emotional anonymity of parallel parenting. You can reduce the impact of television violence on your child either by guiding your child to less violent programming or by discussing any violence in a way that will enable your youngster to process it in light of your personal values.

Parallel play is when a child, usually a preschooler, plays in the same room with other children but does not play interactively with those children. Parallel parenting is a similar concept. The child (of any age) and parent are in the same room, participating in separate activities. The youngster and adult do not interact, do not share feelings, do not engage in a mutually enjoyable activity, and do not acknowledge each other's presence. Parallel parenting leaves children with a sense of being unknown, emotionally anonymous, to the parent. According to author Ron Taffel, this anonymity can turn to rage and aggression.[30] This thought brings us to the next suggestion.

Become actively and meaningfully involved in your child's life. Preadolescents are still willing to spend time with their parents. Take advantage of this while you can. As we will see in the next chapter, a major developmental task for adolescents is to separate from their parents. They will enter a process of individuation that requires them to pull away from you and form intimate relationships with their peers. Therefore, the time to help children create a value system that sees anger as a tool to assert themselves, instead of a weapon for berating themselves and hurting others, needs to be now. This time can be a period of preparation that leads to a positive adolescent experience.

9
Effectively Responding to Angry Adolescents

FOR MORE THAN HALF OF MY PROFESSIONAL CAREER as a counselor, I refused to work with adolescents. During that time, I visited at least three programs for adolescent substance abusers. Each time I left one of those visits, I took with me a vision of TV sets bolted down so they could not be thrown, doors securely locked to contain runaways, and at least one piece of furniture obviously shattered by someone's rage. My impression of adolescents consisted of violent, uncontrollable beings who were not in the least bit motivated to change. Then, in the 1990s, I found myself working at an adolescent substance abuse residential treatment program. I quickly learned that my previous ideas about adolescents were distorted and inaccurate.

Young people between the ages of fourteen and eighteen will start this period at the end of their childhood and, before it is over, transition into adulthood. This is a gigantic developmental move, shifting the adolescent from total dependency upon adults to, if the young person chooses, total independence. The physical, social, and psychological adjustments necessary to achieve this transition are profound.

Successful adjustment in each developmental domain requires anger to perform its intended functions. Along with using anger to bring about these changes, the body produces the chemical origins of fear as a byproduct of the many adjustments the adolescent makes. If not handled properly, the fear is transformed into angry feelings. This produces the potential for extreme amounts of angry feelings to be incurred by a teenager living the average life of an adolescent. The young person who has not been taught the skills necessary for constructive anger is likely to be overwhelmed, appear violent, and act out.

This does not mean that adolescents have a natural tendency to be violent, that they like to be out of control, or that they are unwilling to change. My experience has shown that the opposite is true. They experience extreme remorse after a bout of violence. They feel afraid when out of control. And they cooperatively, willingly at times, modify their behaviors when given clear directions on how to make the requested modifications.

Recently in a group counseling session, a client made a remark that touched a sensitive spot in another client, a person I will call Robert. I looked over at Robert, a teen with a history of hitting his mother until she was unconscious, armed robbery, and discharging firearms in public places. His face was bright red. He appeared agitated and had moved forward in his chair. He lifted his hand and was pointing a finger at the other client as he began to talk. I said, "Stop. Do not point your finger."

Robert put his hand down and looked at me. In a very clipped, anxious tone, he asked, "Can I leave the room? I need to leave." He was still red.

I said, "No, not until you take a deep breath." He did that and I added, "Now, slowly let it out." He did. I watched the red in his face leave; starting with his forehead, it receded to below his chin. I gave another direction, "Tell him what you need to say."

He sat back, looked at the other client, and firmly, without pugnacity, stated, "Don't say that again. Please don't do that to me again."

The other client responded, "Man, I didn't mean anything by it. Honest."

The moment for fighting passed. Both young people looked relieved. They did not have to exchange blows and their public images were preserved.

Robert's ability to comply with specific directions when in such a highly agitated state did not develop in a vacuum and certainly did not occur instantaneously. The staff, along with program guidelines and philosophy, prepared an emotional atmosphere that made his compliance possible.

To create an emotional atmosphere conducive to producing effective responses during anger episodes that involve adolescents, the four basic elements of safety, honesty, respect, and fairness are needed. These elements can be implemented by a teacher in a classroom, a parent in a home, a counselor in a mental health facility, or an athletic coach in a gym. Without them, a constructive response to an adolescent's angry outburst may prove elusive.

Physical safety needs to be the first priority when dealing with potentially angry teens. Studies show that an inordinate number of adolescents who commit violent acts have had extensive exposure to violence either as a witness or as a victim.[1] An adolescent with this type of history sees the world as a dangerous place. This creates a tendency to misinterpret neutral events as physically perilous. The excess of perceived danger requires the person to maintain a defensive posture, ready to fight. Any real threat, no matter how minor, is likely to trigger an aggressive response. Safety, provided by structure and philosophy, helps to counteract this process by allowing overly defensive adolescents to put aside their aggressive guard. The lessons presented by the Zapotec people of Mexico indicate an effective way to accomplish this: Maintain a zero tolerance for violence.[2] Zero tolerance includes threats of violence and any play aggression, commonly known as horseplay, as well as actual acts of physical aggression.

Maintaining a safe environment dictates that alcohol and other drug use be dealt with as soon as suspicions arise. An investigation of the characteristics of adolescents who have committed homicides revealed that 77 percent had a history of alcohol abuse.[3] Another research project that looked into high school students' risk factors for committing violence or being the victim of violence indicated that alcohol and drugs had a significant and positive association with the perpetration of violent acts.[4]

Alcohol and other mood-altering drugs are influential in the production of aggressive behaviors. Therefore, if you want to ensure a safe environment, be alert to the signs of substance abuse. For an adolescent, this includes the following:

- isolation (avoiding family members and old friends)
- a change in image (sometimes a radical alteration in appearance)
- a new set of friends (often older)
- long unsupervised periods of time (skipping school or sneaking out of the house at night)
- physical effects (anxiety, irritability, red eyes, weight loss)

Once alerted, take the necessary actions to obtain a confidential assessment by a certified substance abuse professional. Then follow the professional's suggestions.

Honesty is crucial when developing a relationship of trust. This is especially true when interacting with adolescents, where it becomes a paramount ingredient to nondefensive, nonaggressive communication. Being honest does not mean that you have to divulge your deepest, darkest, most sensitive secrets to the nearest teenager. It is helpful, however, for young people to have clear information about issues that involve their lives.

The majority of adolescents are astute and sensitive to their surroundings. They can tell when something is up, and it does not take them long to know when they have been told a lie. Once recognized, the lie becomes a trigger for intense anger. When asked about the angry feeling, they point to the adult's hypocrisy. Adolescents judge lies as an extreme form of disrespect.

Respect is one of the most valued commodities to a teenager. A common answer given by high-school-aged youth, when asked what triggered a violent episode, is, "They dissed me." Adolescents are willing to fight when they think they have been shown disrespect. And the corollary is just as true: Adolescents are willing to cooperate when they think they have been shown respect. The guidelines for doing this are simple. Show them the same courtesies and socially appropriate behaviors as you would an adult. Listen closely, without interruptions; verbalize value to the young person's feelings and opinions; actively show that you are open to considering new ideas; when you are wrong, admit it; and when you are right, stand firm.

Fairness is important, especially to an adolescent. With that said, I must add a caution. Be careful that your personal need to be fair does not outweigh your good judgment. Always keep in mind that safety and age appropriateness take precedence over fairness. Make decisions that are consistent and well thought out rather than inconsistent and whimsical. As young people get older, they need room for more freedom and possible negotiations. When fairness is recognized as a mainstay of the relationship between you and the adolescent, fewer arguments and resultant angry feelings will be generated by the adolescent battle cry of "That's not fair!"

The elements of safety, honesty, respect, and fairness provide an atmosphere of emotional security. During the age range of fourteen to eighteen, this piece of emotional safety may be the only secure anchor in the adolescent's world. As the preparation for adulthood begins, progresses, and comes to fruition, every aspect of life seems to be turning upside down and inside out. This is natural because, for young people, the most predominant and important developmental task is individuation, the separation of the child from the parental figures in order to become a distinct individual. During this process, everything inside and outside seems to change. All of these changes can affect or be affected by anger. The most apparent and potentially difficult maturational processes can be addressed in such a manner that anger becomes an asset to adolescent development, as well as personal relationships.

PHYSICAL MATURATION

Although young people are probably through puberty by the time this stage begins, the body is still undergoing profound physical changes, and their hormones and other growth-producing chemicals are still in flux, at times seemingly out of control. Young men will bulk up and young women will shape out. Both males and females may experience extreme physical awkwardness at this time, as though they have lost control of their bodies and remaining upright on both feet is a chore. They will have a great deal of concern about being attractive to others.

As discussed in chapter 3, the body's chemicals, especially hormones, determine a person's emotions. Adolescents undergo severe hormonal changes, with resultant emotional ups and downs. One minute they can be hyper, with excessive energy-producing anger, and the next minute they appear drained and depressed. They can be happy preparing breakfast and pouting by the time they get to the table for cereal.

When the young people get to seventeen or eighteen years old, the physical changes begin to ease, and they have more physical control and a fuller understanding of their own bodies. The emotional moodiness is less pronounced.

While adolescents are going through this phase, the adults in their lives can make use of several interventions to minimize the potential for destructive anger.

SLOWING DOWN THE HIGH ENERGY

During the high-energy periods, when you see the anger begin to build, you need to help your adolescent slow down. To do that, you need to be slowed down. The one obstacle with a strong potential to deter this approach is the adult tendency to interpret the adolescent's anger as a judgment of their role. Mothers and fathers often react to the teen's anger as if it's saying, "You are a bad parent." The teacher may hear it as, "You are a lousy teacher."

To respond constructively, you need to interrupt these interpretations. The quick relaxation exercise practiced in chapter 5, combined with directive self-talk, can achieve this. To successfully use this approach, your self-talk would go like this:

- STOP, STOP, STOP
- Take a deep breath, one, two, three.
- Slowly let it out. RELAX.
- This anger is not about me. It is his. I'll direct him on how to slow it all down.

Then say to the adolescent: "Take a breath. Slow down. I can listen better when you slow down."

Practice this mentally by remembering an incident of anger when the adolescent had high energy and you were able to watch the anger escalate. During your relaxation session, mentally relive that incident, inserting the relaxation and self-talk into the mental picture at the spot where you notice the teen's energy increasing.

A Good Time to Talk

At around the age of fourteen, teenagers begin individuation by pulling away from their "uncool" parents and moving toward their peers. But there will continue to be times when teens are available to their parents. Often these times occur during their moping, pouting periods. Parents see the young person moping and, wanting to connect with their child, ask, "What's wrong?" At that moment, with hormones wreaking emotional havoc, the teen thinks everything is wrong. And so she answers, "Nothing." End of conversation.

Teens commonly have two characteristics, however, that can open the door to extended, and sometimes very meaningful, conversations:

- Thinking no one understands them, they want to be understood.
- They enjoy sharing information that is important to them.

Working with teenagers, I soon realized I have no idea of how it feels to be an adolescent today. I do not know what it is like to get up five days a week to attend a school where the student next to me may have a weapon, or where there may be a bomb in the bathroom, or where someone might go crazy and shoot my favorite teacher. I do not know what feelings I would experience being sixteen years old and being searched every school day for a weapon, or approached to buy drugs, or prodded into a fight. I do not know what I would do at the age of fifteen facing fads that include pierced tongues, pink hair, and tattoos. I know at least one adolescent who does, and since you are reading this chapter, I think it a safe bet that you do, too. Your teenager wants you to ask and wants you to listen. Below are some questions that will help your teen talk to you. I suggest that you preface your queries by acknowledging your lack of expertise.

- What are the most difficult parts of your day?
- Do you ever think what happened at Columbine could happen in your school?
- What is it like at your school?

In the past two weeks, events have occurred in your area that could affect your teenager. Daily, the national news reports situations that involve teenagers. Think of three incidents from the local or national news that provide questions to ask your child. It is important that you phrase the questions so they do not sound like you are making an accusation or conducting an inquisition.

Incident #1:

Question:

Incident #2:

Question:

Incident #3:

Question:

VALUES IDENTIFICATION

Many young people enter adolescence with vague personal values. They have ideas of what is right and wrong. Unfortunately, with most of these ideas being black and white, they are not always realistic. As teenagers progress through these years, their ability to think in the abstract grows. When this development occurs, they can stretch beyond the concrete values of childhood into more moral and philosophical principles.

Again, because individuation requires young people to strive for autonomy, their quest to create a personal set of values may begin with the active rejection of parental values. The peer group, with its values, norms, and mores, becomes the young person's guiding force for determining socially acceptable and appropriate behavior. Social bonding occurs and anger is generated to protect the group's tenets. A typical "we" vs. "they" scenario is set in motion. The more your preferences and values conflict with those of the adolescent "we" group, the greater the teen resists, often in the form of anger. Unless you want to be doing constant battle with your child, it is important that you are clear on your values and how they coincide with the peer group's values, and that you know which of your values you are willing to let go of, which ones you are willing to compromise, and which ones you will stand firm on.

An example of a value you might be willing to let go of is the adolescent's mode of dress. The current teen trend may not be to your liking, but is there an indecent amount of flesh showing? If not, in the arena of modesty this is more decent than what my generation wore. This is a battle that you might be willing to forgo.

I have a close friend who currently is trying to raise two teens. He is an avid jazz fan and abhors the music his son likes. So they negotiated an agreement about how the son can listen to the music of his peer group: His son is to spend his own money on that type of music. Also, since my friend does not want to hear the music, his son needs to listen to it in a way that does not spill into his father's hearing space.

Examples of what you would stand firm on and become assertive about include anything that is unsafe or illegal or harmful to others.

Picking Your Battles

Now that you have the categories clear, you need to know what specific behaviors go into each category. Think of conflicts, or potential conflicts, that have arisen between you and your teen. Place each under the heading of the category that it belongs in.

Let go	Negotiate	Stand firm

Keeping within Your Limits

Once you have determined the areas that are negotiable, know what you want out of the negotiations. In the example of my friend and his son, he knew that he would not pay for the music and he knew that he did not want to hear the music. On each of the negotiable items that you listed above, what is the minimum that you want from the negotiations?

Negotiable item #1:
Minimum wants:

Negotiable item #2:
Minimum wants:

Negotiable item #3:
Minimum wants:

Negotiable item #4:
Minimum wants:

Clarify Values from Rules

One day in my mid-twenties, shortly after Christmas, I had an epiphany. A friend had given me a beautiful, wonderful tennis racket. I wanted very much to try it out. There was snow and ice on the ground outside. I looked around the living room and thought, "Maybe I could just bounce one off the wall." A strong, firm voice in the back of my head said, "Don't play ball in the house!" And I started to wonder, "Why not?" This was not the first time I had thought that question. But now, I had it as an inquiring adult and not a whiny, angry child who could not have her way. And the answer was simple: "I might break something." I looked around the room and realized that everything fragile was mine and I could either do without or replace anything I might break. I pushed the furniture aside and spent at least an hour practicing my forehand.

What my parents had never made clear is that the rule is not the value. A rule is developed to protect a value. They did not want their possessions broken and they probably did not want noise invading their quiet time. The value, consideration for others' property and territory, was the important element, not the rule. The value would go with me the rest of my life. The rule was only applicable in given situations. I could even change the rule, as long as the value was not at issue or continued to be protected using another method.

Separating Values and Rules

Anger is especially strong when employed to protect values. When rules replace values, angry feelings may be triggered to protect rules as though they are values. Another important difference between rules and values is the negotiability of each. Most rules can be negotiated, whereas most values cannot. Therefore, it is important to know whether rules or values are presenting conflict between you and your adolescent. Also, as you and your young person talk about values during this phase, notice that even though teens may have originally rejected parental values, probability is high that they will return to those values as they pass through the last part of this phase.

Below, list the rules that you and your adolescent argue about the most. Then indicate the value being protected by the rule. Note any possible ways to maintain the value while modifying the rule.

Rule: _____ Value: _____
Potential modification: _____

Rule: _____ Value: _____
Potential modification: _____

Rule: _____ Value: _____
Potential modification: _____

Rule: _____ Value: _____
Potential modification: _____

IDENTITY SOLIDIFICATION

Before entering adolescence, children look to their family for validation and identity. Once into adolescence, individuation forces young people to seek identity beyond the confines of familial parameters. During the early part of this phase, adolescents naturally tend to be mercurial, changing identity as they encounter different groups and different friends. Although they want to be seen as special, even unique, the need to belong leads young teens to avoid being different. Their worth and sense of self is derived from others.

By the end of adolescence, however, most of these characteristics change. Older teens are less influenced by peers as they develop a stronger sense of self. Although comparisons to others may influence their personal identity, this comparison is more realistically based. Older adolescents no longer move from group to group, friend to friend. Even with many friend-ships, they maintain a steady persona as they drift between groups or from one friend to another.

The psychological protection function of anger does extra duty during adolescence as it works to defend the individual's fluid identity. The self-messages, evaluating the young person with comparisons to others, are sen-sitively close to the surface. The angry defensiveness is used to save the teen's personal image when one of the predominant negative self-messages is activated. Of the many negative self-evaluations that are possible, four seem to be universal for adolescents:

- I'm not good enough.
- I'm not important.
- I'm worthless.
- I'm wrong.

Adolescents believe these messages and fear you and/or others will dis-cover them. Anger is generated to keep them hidden. When this occurs, a nonthreatening response directed at the message can encourage the negative evaluation to surface and assuage the angry façade. For me, the easiest way to be nonthreatening is to present the underlying message I think I have heard in the form of a question. "John, are you saying that I think you are not good enough?" Or, "Mary, are you saying that I think you are not im-portant?" "Do you think my suggestion meant that you are worthless?" An answer in the affirmative opens the door for discussion. If the answer is no, you have two valid ways to go: "I'm glad, because I would not want you to get that idea." Or, "Oh, okay, how did you interpret what I was saying?" At this point the anger recedes and we can begin a meaningful conversation.

Responding to Negative Self-Messages

In order to respond effectively to negative self-messages, there are two tenets that need to be remembered:

- The spoken words are the opposite of the message beneath the anger.
- The anger has little to do with you. It is the manifestation of the ado-lescent's struggle to come to terms with personal identity.

Because of this, it is very helpful to use your quick relaxation technique and self-talk to focus, in preparation to respond. It would mentally sound like this:

- STOP, STOP, STOP.
- Take a deep breath, count to three.
- RELAX.
- This is _____'s anger. It's not about me. Let me listen.

Once you have completed practicing the quick relaxation, fill in the following blank areas to prepare for when you need to use this type of response.

Remember the last time the adolescent was angry:

What were some of the things the adolescent said? Use specific words and phrases.

What might have been the adolescent's self-message?

How could you respond to bring that message to the surface?

Remember a previous time when the adolescent was angry:

What were some of the things the adolescent said? Use specific words and phrases.

What might have been the adolescent's self-message?

How could you respond to bring that message to the surface?

What is another time when the adolescent was especially angry?

What were some of the things the adolescent said? Use specific words and phrases.

What might have been the adolescent's self-message?

How could you respond to bring that message to the surface?

Review each of the above incidents. Envision the incident and your new response. Then imagine what the adolescent's reply will be and how you will respond to that.

Incident #1:

Your first response:

The adolescent's reply:

Your next response:

Incident #2:

Your first response:

The adolescent's reply:

Your next response:

Incident #3

Your first response:

The adolescent's reply:

Your next response:

    During your next relaxation session, practice these responses by re-viewing the above scenarios in your mind while relaxed.

NO ADVICE GIVING!

Your teenage daughter storms in, ranting about something that happened at school with a friend. She turns to you and asks, "Well, what would you do?" As inviting as it may seem, do not step into that trap!

Many of you already may have discovered the pitfalls involved in giving advice to an adolescent. If your advice was not solicited, the anger appears within the first sentence. If your advice was sought, the teen shows signs of irritation after the second sentence and may have shut down mentally by the fourth. Your advice may be wonderful and, in fact, may be the best reasoning that anyone could ever have for someone of your age. It is the age difference that causes the problem. An adolescent's priorities can be very different from those of an adult. What is so right for you is far down the list for the teen. When she hears your way, and it is far removed from her possible solutions, the young person tends to internalize it as, "I'm wrong again," activating a major negative self-evaluation.

A good way to avoid the advice-giving trap is through the use of Socratic questions. Socrates thought the right questions lead people to find the answer right for them. I encourage you to have that same level of conviction with the adolescent in your life. For the following approach to work, your belief that the teenager is capable of finding a solution appropriate and meaningful for an adolescent's lifestyle is essential. Without that belief, your questions will sound hypocritical and condescending.

When your teen asks, "What would you do?" your first question is: *What ideas have you come up with?*

When the adolescent presents an idea or two, for each one ask: *What could happen if you do that?*

When an answer is given, ask: *What do you gain from that? What are the risks?*

When that is completed for each option, ask: *Are you sure you do not have any more ideas?*

When all the ideas are laid out, the gains and risks compared, ask the adolescent: *Which one is best for you?*

If the adolescent settles on an option that is physically unsafe, you need to ask: *That does not sound safe to me. How can you make it safe?* Do not support a solution that is physically risky.

If your teen answers your first question—What ideas have you come up with?—using the adolescent's favorite response, "Nothing," your question becomes: *So we've got either doing nothing or doing something. If you move over to the something side, what do you suppose is the worst thing you could do?*

After the teen gives you an answer, ask: *What would be a little better than that?*

Then ask: *Can you think of anything even better than that?*

Finally, ask: *Is there anything wrong with that?*

If the answer is no, fine. If the answer points out a problem within the solution, ask: *Do you have any ideas on how to overcome that?*

If, during either of these questioning processes, you sound judgmental or critical toward the young person's responses, the negative self-messages will be triggered and anger will be generated for protection.

Becoming Socrates

Both of the processes, as written above, are shown using my words. You probably have a different style of speaking and therefore would word the questions differently.

To clarify in your mind each process, think of an incident when you gave advice. How could you have answered using the first process?

Initial question to discover the adolescent's ideas:

For each option, ask

Outcome question:

Gains question:

Risks question:

Verification of no more options:

Solution question:

How could you have answered using the second process?

Initial question to discover adolescent's ideas:

Initial worst thing question:

A little better question:

Anything even better question:

Investigate for problems:

Solutions question:

Do not compromise on safety!

In either of these two processes, if anything seems dangerous or unsafe, how will you guide the adolescent to a safer solution with questions?

EMOTIONAL CONNECTIONS

Children move along a relatively clear, progressively intense path of emotional involvement with other people. For preadolescents, relationships are mostly of the same sex and revolve around an activity of mutual interest. Adolescents, on the other hand, do not need a specific activity of interest to generate mutuality. They can talk for long periods of time, jumping from one topic to another. As any parent can attest, adolescents can be on the phone for hours or spend most of an evening in an Internet chat room. They are involved in the developmental task of discovering and exploring the first stage of intimacy, self-disclosure. They may share thoughts, feelings, future plans, fantasies, and experiences. In early adolescence, the conversations are usually with close friends of the same sex. However, some fourteen-year-olds will participate in the more mature relationship structuring employed by older adolescents as they seek intimacy with people they are sexually attracted to. Whether friendship or romance, the relationships of the later part of adolescence are usually pairs or couples.

This being the case, the teenage years comprise a time of best friends and first lovers. Once teens begin self-disclosing, their capacity to move into more intimate conversations, those that come from a vulnerable emotional level, occurs and expands the depth of the relational experience. An adolescent who does not understand the dynamics of anger, especially its functions, and who does not have the ability to experience and use basic emotions, will be hindered when attempting to master this piece of maturation.

An Anger Journal

I was having a difficult time thinking of an exercise that would provide adults with a method to help adolescents learn about feelings. So, as I passed by five teenagers who were sitting around in our group therapy room waiting for the counselor, I joined them and asked, "How could your parents have helped you learn about feelings?"

Their responses came quickly. They barely needed time to think. "They could have talked to us about them." "They could have shared their feelings."

"Suppose they didn't know how because they hadn't been taught?" I asked.

The newest client in the group shrugged her shoulders and, in a very matter-of-fact voice, replied, "Then they couldn't help us."

Giving credence to their responses, the first task for parents would be to learn the functions of anger—how it is used and how the dynamic connection between fear and anger operates in daily situations.

Keep an anger journal for five days. At the end of each day list the angry incidents that you witnessed (include watching someone's anger when you are not involved, experiencing your own anger, and being the target of another person's anger). How was the anger used or misused? (Reviewing chapter 2 may be helpful.) What fear or threat do you think the anger was protecting?

<u>Anger Incidents</u>	<u>How Used or Misused</u>	<u>Fear or Threat</u>
Day One		
Day Two		
Day Three		
Day Four		
Day Five		

The tendency of some adults to view adolescent anger as an accusation or a show of disrespect hampers their ability to effectively respond to that anger and assist teens in finding ways to use angry feelings constructively. Therefore, it is important to remember that the teenager's anger is generated by fear or by a perceived threat also. And the most effective means for defusing an angry outburst so that you can have a discussion is to address the fear openly. This is simple to do because adolescents are relatively transparent in their fears.

To target the fear, when the adolescent makes a statement that sounds accusatory, add the words *I'm afraid* to the front of the sentence. For example, the teen says, "It doesn't matter. *You don't care.*" The accusatory statement, "You don't care," becomes the fear statement, *I'm afraid you don't care.*

To address the fear openly, make the phrase into a question and ask, *Are you afraid I don't care?* Once that is out in the open, you can respond to the fear.

Responding to the Fear

Think over the past week, remembering incidents that involved an adolescent's anger. What was the accusatory statement in each incident? What would the fear statement be? How would you form a question to help bring the fear out into the open?

Angry incident #1:

Accusatory statement:

Fear statement:

Opening question:

Angry incident #2:

Accusatory statement:

Fear statement:

Opening question:

Angry incident #3:

Accusatory statement:

Fear statement:

Opening question:

Angry incident #4:

Accusatory statement:

Fear statement:

Opening question:

EMERGING INDEPENDENCE

As I said before, parents tell me that there are two age periods in their children's lives that they wish they could have avoided. I call these time periods the terrible Ts—the terrible twos and the terrible teens. Looking beyond the sophistication level in functioning and developmental tasks, these two phases have many similarities. They are times of increased autonomy, with incremental separation from caregivers as a major developmental task. Both the toddler and the early adolescent typically want to do more than their capabilities allow. Frustration and power struggles between child and parent follow.

There is another similarity that may be encouraging to some. The earlier developmental stages have an impact on how children deal with frustration and power struggles. Just as a toddler's days are less defiant if caregivers helped the child learn to self-regulate during infancy, the teen years can be less aggressively defiant if the youngster has not been disciplined with corporal punishment. Here is where you receive the payoff for the numerous times during your child's earlier years that, with sheer force of will, you refrained from following through on that urge to smack him one. It is most likely true that the smack would have produced immediate conformity. The eventual side effects would appear in the adolescent stage as increased defiance, anger, and a higher probability of violence.[5]

That does not mean you cannot respond constructively and helpfully to your teen's anger if she was physically punished as a child. It just means that your efforts may be a little more taxing than those of the caregiver of an adolescent who was not disciplined with physical force. No matter what type of early discipline was used, the developmental tasks for adults and the adolescents during this phase remain the same. They revolve around the young person's preparation for adulthood.

A major task for adults in preparing teens to assume the responsibilities of adulthood is to relinquish power safely, in ways that are age appropriate. During this exchange of power, the adolescent's task is to demonstrate increasing amounts of responsible behavior. Power, how individuals view it and how they abuse it, has a strong influence on determining a person's angry feelings and behavioral expression of those feelings. Therefore, the most vehement, often aggressive conflicts arise from when adults are unable to let go of appropriate amounts of power or teens attempt to gain power they are not capable of handling safely.

It is up to the adults to ensure that power is exchanged safely and to respond constructively to any expressions of anger by the adolescent. The three elements necessary for successfully accomplishing this are flexible planning, limit setting, and relationship maintenance.

Flexible Planning

Flexible planning asks that you make a plan of when you will allow the adolescent more power, which for the adolescent usually means more freedom. This power, or freedom, is the condition placed at the ending of the thought, "I will let him drive the car when he _____." The filler phrase here might be, "has a job and can pay the additional insurance."

Below, fill in the sentence's first blank space with the piece of power, or freedom, that you need to exchange with the teen. Fill in the second blank space with the responsible behavior that you think indicates the adolescent's readiness for that exchange.

I will let my teenager _____

_____

when _____

_____

I will let my teenager _____

_____

when _____

_____

I will let my teenager _____

_____

when _____

_____

I will let my teenager _____

_____

when _____

_____

I will let my teenager _____

_____

when _____

_____

Once you are satisfied with the plan to exchange power with your adolescent, I encourage you to discuss it together. Except for matters that involve safety, allow room for negotiation. Also, your teen may desire certain pieces of autonomy that you did not consider. Seek your adolescent's input on how you might know whether she is responsible enough to handle the suggested freedom.

Limit Setting

Limit setting can have a number of meanings. In this instance, I am referring to placing behavioral limits on the expression of anger. Personally, I can tolerate any expression of anger that is not verbally or physically aggressive or violent. Culture and individual circumstances dictate what behavioral limits you will set. Once you have determined those limits, stick to them by using natural and logical consequences.

Natural and logical consequences are the results that normally occur from a particular action. Communities have laws that regulate specific behaviors and social conventions that outline the actions needed to mend a situation. Parents can guide their teens by letting them experience the natural consequences of their actions or devise logical consequences that stem from that action. Examples of natural and logical consequences would be:

- If I am physically attacked, I file assault and battery charges.
- If you intentionally break the furniture, you fix it or replace it.
- If you demonstrate anger in a healthy, assertive way, I will consider your request and help you find a positive way to achieve what you want.

Notice that the consequence has meaning because it is related to the specific situation or to the real world. Earlier in this chapter, I talked about the adolescent's sensitivity to fairness. This approach contains a fairness that teenagers clearly understand and respond well to.

Determining Consequences

Below list the limits that indicate unacceptable expressions of anger. Then indicate potential logical consequences.

Unacceptable anger expression:

Logical consequence:

Unacceptable anger expression:

Logical consequence:

Unacceptable anger expression:

Logical consequence:

Unacceptable anger expression:

Logical consequence:

Unacceptable anger expression:

Logical consequence:

Unacceptable anger expression:

Logical consequence:

Maintain a Relationship

Throughout the struggle for autonomy and power between the adult and the adolescent, it is important to maintain a relationship that has meaning on an emotional level. Emotions tie people together and maintain their relationships, especially through difficult times. Often the focus of attention, and resultant conflict, is placed on behaviors created by the tug-of-war that occurs when teens get frustrated because freedoms are not bestowed at their whim and will. To defuse the conflict, move to a response that presents how you feel.[6]

Many years ago, I was doing a two-day workshop to train secretaries on how to respond to angry outbursts from customers. One of the participants repeatedly wanted to discuss her sixteen-year-old daughter. It seems that the daughter was "always late." The teen would come in late, the mother would yell, and the teen yelled back. This scene happened three times a week. I found out from the woman that her concern with her daughter's tardiness was that she feared her daughter would be hurt. She added that she would not mind the adolescent's lateness as long as she knew her daughter was safe. The woman decided she would try sharing her fears with her daughter the next time she was late. That evening, her daughter was a half-hour late. The young woman entered the kitchen, as usual, and belligerently began defending her tardiness. The woman turned to her daughter and, in a voice that matched her feeling, said, "When you are late, I am so afraid that something bad has happened to you." She reported that her daughter was speechless, so she added, "Maybe we can work something out so I am not afraid."

I never found out the complete outcome to this woman's efforts because that was the last day of the workshop. I do know that for at least one evening she and her daughter reconnected.

The feeling we express to our teens does not always have to be fear. It could be guilt, sadness, loneliness, or inadequacy. When we experience and express any of our feelings, except anger, we invite the adolescent to communicate on a level that bypasses the argumentative anger.

Connecting Emotionally

Pick three major conflicts that you experience regularly with your adolescent. What feeling, besides anger, was triggering your behavior? What statement could you have made to express that feeling?

Conflict:

Your feeling:

Feeling statement:

Conflict:

Your feeling:

Feeling statement:

Conflict:

Your feeling:

Feeling statement:

One of the simplest yet most powerful things adults can do to enhance their relationships with their adolescents is to admit mistakes. Between the years of fourteen and eighteen, most young people discover that their parents have flaws, make errors, break promises, and do not know all the answers. As this reality sinks in, teenagers can experience intense anger. Their worldview and security has been shaken. Since they already know you are not God, there is no harm when you stop acting as though you ought to be. Admitting a mistake not only shows the adult's humanity, it also demonstrates for the adolescent that mistakes can be made without fearing terrible repercussions. It also gives teenagers permission to talk about their mistakes.

Once you admit a mistake, another relationship-building endeavor is to ask for help in determining how the mistake can be remedied. This is especially necessary if the mistake caused harm to the teen. To do otherwise, to defend or ignore the error, leaves the young person with intense anger and you as the target. This type of approach shows the adolescent that, not only is he held accountable for wrongs and their consequences, so are you.

Admitting mistakes and sharing emotions help build an atmosphere of trust and fairness. This atmosphere can be very important to adolescents. As they seek greater personal power and independence, their recognition of these areas of equality and similarity will reduce their need to act out aggressively to obtain them.

10

There Is a Time

FOR MANY PEOPLE, the goal of aggression is to equalize power by showing physical superiority when they sense inequity in other domains. When this is the case, violence becomes a demonstration of power. The perpetrator of the violent behavior succeeds only when the victim cannot physically defend against the onslaught. Physically aggressive behavior, therefore, generally flows downward from the stronger to the weaker. This is also true for verbal and emotional aggression. Authoritarian strength works like physical strength.

When these types of abuse occur, individuals on the receiving end need to protect themselves. For potential physical harm, defense is best achieved by leaving the scene immediately. When this is not possible, victims need to find a way out as soon as possible. This may require that they use their own anger to implement a plan of action.

A TIME TO FLEE

Keep yourself safe. Warning signs can indicate when someone is verging on violent behavior. If you are in an argument or a discussion, these following signs may indicate you are in an unsafe situation and need to leave:

- The angry person has been using mood-altering substances.
- The angry person calls you dehumanizing names. The name-calling continues after you have asked that it stop.
- You are familiar with this person's pattern of aggression and you know from experience that the behaviors are escalating into a violent episode.

The above warning signs are not all inclusive. Some aggressive people have other specific signs that they are about to erupt. There may be someone in your life, either now or when you were a child, who periodically acted out aggressively. What were some signs that preceded the violent behavior? If that person is still a part of your life, what do you need to do to leave, and how will you leave the situation when you see the indicators? When will it be safe for you to return?

Signs of Potential Violence
These are the signs that tell me violence is possible:

Preparations to Leave
This is what I need to do in case the signs of potential violence appear:

Escape Plan
This is how I will leave:

This is where I will go:

I will stay there until:

SEEKING PROFESSIONAL ASSISTANCE

When family members express anger in the form of abuse or battering, they need professional help. The emotional ties that hold a family together can make it almost impossible for one family member to help another when violent expressions of anger are the problem. Spouse and child abuse, as well as sibling violence, require the help of a professional. Physical abuse, once committed, occurs again unless intervened on and addressed with appropriate therapeutic help.[1]

If you have been the victim of abuse, seek professional help. Even though you may think leaving or seeking professional help will create an unsafe situation, contacting your local mental health clinic or social services agency will provide a number of options that are available to you for your safety.

The same is true for a child suffering the trauma of physical or emotional abuse. The long-term effects can be devastating, not only to the child but also to significant others and society in general as the child matures. Again, a local social services agency or mental health clinic are places to begin when searching to find professional assistance for young people victimized by physical or emotional abuse.

INVOKING YOUR ANGER FOR CHANGE

The major sections of this workbook have focused on responding to other people's anger by using defusion techniques, employing responses that encourage intimacy, or providing the means to help children and adolescents express their anger productively. At this point you may be thinking: "I have tried all the things you suggested. They work for a while and then there is another flare-up."

There is a time, when you have sincerely tried and failed, that moving on is the most viable alternative. Moving on means different things depending upon the situation. With children, adolescents, and, at times, spouses, it means moving to the next step to seek professional intervention.

There are circumstances where moving on means finding a way to leave or ameliorate the situation. An example might be an employment setting that includes an explosive boss. Or perhaps your landlord or neighbors are antagonistic. When the cost of another person's anger exceeds what you receive from the relationship, it is time to invoke your anger to provide the motivation necessary for change.

Using anger as a motivation for change requires that you express your anger assertively. Many people think assertive anger means that a person experiences the anger arousal and expresses the angry feeling immediately, and then the incident is finished. An assertive response style, however, involves the action necessary to fulfill your needs, without intentionally detracting from the needs of another. Most of the time this requires more than a single event. A successful assertive response usually involves a process that consists of a series of events. For example, if you decide to leave a job because the atmosphere is hostile, you will need to decide what new job you want, determine whether you have the necessary qualifications, gain any required credentials, investigate potential employment openings, and follow necessary steps for application. Anger can supply the energy to accomplish all of this and more.

First you need to decide where you want to focus your anger. To do this, complete the following plan.

What is the situation that I need to move on from?

Where do I want to move on to?

To get there, I need
    1.
    2.
    3.
    4.
    5.
    6.

My plan for obtaining these needs is
    1.
    2.
    3.
    4.
    5.
    6.

I will initiate this plan on:

The plan that you developed may seem overwhelming. Use your anger to achieve it one piece at a time. Two of the greatest characteristics of constructively expressed anger are the additional strength and the steadiness of direction it provides during times of adversity. To invoke and use these aspects of anger:

- Visualize the situation that convinced you to move on.
- Relive that event in your mind.
- Allow yourself to feel and use the energy produced by focusing on the next step of the plan.

After you have achieved one or two steps of the plan, you may discover that the energy from the old anger-producing incident is waning. That is not usually a problem. Once you've accomplished the first step, other motivators become available, such as the realization that you can accomplish the increments necessary to reach the goal, the positive sense of yourself that accompanies success, or the emotional support from others as they become a part of your new life. When anger triggers constructive ideas of how to move away from situations maintained by destructive expressions of anger, the action itself takes on power and a life of its own. The plan, initiated by anger in response to anger, acquires new motivators, usually provided by its success, to sustain its continued application.

If you are being abused, please understand that

- It is not your fault.
- You cannot make the abuser change his or her behavior.
- You are not alone. There are people who can help. You can call the National Resource Center on Domestic Violence (1-800-537-2238) or the Resource Center for Child Custody and Protection (1-800-527-3223).

$\mathcal{N}otes$

Chapter 1: Personal Responses to Another's Anger

1. Klaus Minde, "Aggression in Preschoolers: Its Relation to Socialization," *Journal of American Academy of Child and Adolescent Psychiatry* 31:5 (1992): 853–62, reviews a number of studies concerned with the stability of aggression over time. The idea that aggressive adolescents were aggressive children is often cited as proof of aggression's behavioral stability. When viewed in reverse, these studies indicate that a small percentage of aggressive children develop into violent teenagers, demonstrating the instability of aggression.

2. John R. Marshall, "The Expression of Feelings," *Archives of General Psychiatry* 27 (1972): 786–90.

3. Aron W. Siegman, "Cardiovascular Consequences of Expressing, Experiencing, and Repressing Anger," *Journal of Behavioral Medicine* 16:6 (1993): 539–69, reviews biophysiological experiments done in the 1980s and 1990s that focus on the effects different types of anger expression have on internal reactions, specifically the cardiovascular system.

Chapter 2: The Many Uses and Misuses of Anger

1. Norma D. Feshbach and Kiki Roe, "Empathy in Six- and Seven-Year-Olds," *Child Development* 39 (1968): 133–45.

2. John R. Marshall, "The Expression of Feelings," *Archives of General Psychiatry* 27 (1972): 786–90.

3. Aron W. Siegman, "Cardiovascular Consequences of Expressing, Experiencing, and Repressing Anger," *Journal of Behavioral Medicine* 16:6 (1993): 539–69.

4. Harvey A. Hornstein, *Cruelty and Kindness: A New Look at Aggression and Altruism* (Englewood Cliffs, N.J.: Prentice-Hall, 1976), 13–31, describes his studies on the phenomenon of "we" vs. "they" attitudes and how these manifest in normal, daily situations.

Chapter 3: The Complex Nature of Anger

1. Edmund Jacobson, *Biology of Emotions* (Springfield, Ill.: Charles C. Thomas, 1967), presents a more detailed explanation of the physiology of emotions in general. Angela Scarpa and Adrian Raine, "Psychophysiology of Anger and Violent Behavior," *The Psychiatric Clinics of North America* 20:2 (1997): 375–94, explains the physiology of anger specifically.

2. Albert Bandura, *Aggression: A Social Learning Analysis* (Englewood Cliffs, N.J.: Prentice-Hall, 1973), explains the process involved in learning when and how to express angry feelings. Carol Tavris, *Anger: The Misunderstood Emotion* (New York: Simon & Schuster, 1982), discusses how different cultures around the world place limits on and develop guidelines for the expression of anger.

3. Eric Fidler, "Antisocial Behavior in Boys Studied," America Online, Associated Press (January 13, 2000), reports that a study of boys aged seven to twelve indicated the most aggressive boys had the lowest levels of cortisol. Scarpa and Raine, "Psychophysiology of Anger and Violent Behavior," presents a technical explanation of cortisol's connection to aggression by reviewing a number of studies.

4. Kenneth A. Dodge and Nicki R. Crick, "Social Information-Processing Bases of Aggressive Behavior in Children," *Personality and Social Psychology* 16:1 (1990): 8–22, explains the social information processing (SIP) theory of aggression in children by comparing it to previous theories of aggression.

5. Bahr Weis et al., "Some Consequences of Early Harsh Discipline: Child Aggression and a Maladaptive Social Information Processing Style," *Child Development* 63 (1992): 1321–35, investigates three hypotheses. Relevant to this citation were tests measuring the relationships between SIP and child aggression that indicate greater child aggression related to greater hostile attributional biases (1327).

6. Dodge and Crick, "Social Information-Processing," 13–14.

7. Fidler, "Antisocial Behavior in Boys Studied."

8. Jacobson, *Biology of Emotions*.

9. Albert Bandura, Dorothea Ross, and Sheila A. Ross, "Imitation of Film-Mediated Aggressive Models," *Journal of Abnormal and Social Psychology* 66 (1963): 3–11.

10. Mark I. Singer et al., "Contributors to Violent Behavior among Elementary and Middle School Children," *Pediatrics* 104:4 (1999): 878–84.

Chapter 4: Problems That Can Occur with Anger

1. Li-yu Song, Mark I. Singer, and Trina M. Anglin, "Violence Exposure and Emotional Trauma as Contributors to Adolescents' Violent Behaviors," *Archives of Pediatric and Adolescent Medicine* 152 (1998): 531–36, claims that anger is not only a residual feeling of victimization but the most prevalent symptom of trauma experienced by adolescents.

2. Norma D. Feshbach and Kiki Roe, "Empathy in Six- and Seven-Year-Olds," *Child Development* 39 (1968): 133–45.

3. George Will, "This Week," American Broadcasting Corporation (March 5, 2000).

4. Marvin K. Malek, Bei-Hung Chang, and Terry C. Davis, "Fighting and Weapon-Carrying among Seventh Grade Students in Massachusetts and Louisiana," *Journal of Adolescent Health* 23:2 (1998): 94–102, concludes that parental attitudes concerning violence determine a child's proclivity to fight and/or to carry weapons to school.

Chapter 5: The Foundation

1. Larry Fritzlan, "Raising the Bottom: Setting Limits for Teenage Substance Abusers," *Networker* (July/August 1999): 61.

2. Raymond W. Novaco, "Stress Inoculation: A Cognitive Therapy for Anger and Its Application to a Case of Depression," *Journal of Consulting and Clinical Psychology* 47 (1977): 600–08, shows that self-talk can be used effectively with different emotional states.

Chapter 6: Defusion Techniques

1. Harvey A. Hornstein, *Cruelty and Kindness: A New Look at Aggression and Altruism* (Englewood Cliffs, N.J.: Prentice-Hall, 1976), 13–31.

2. Ronald J. Prinz, Elaine A. Blechman, and Jean E. Dumas, "An Evaluation of Peer Coping Skills Training for Childhood Aggression," *Journal of Clinical Child Psychology* 23:2 (1994): 193–203. Robert N. Jamison, E. Warren Lambert, and Danny J. McCloud, "Social Skills Training with Hospitalized Adolescents: An Evaluative Experiment," *Adolescence* 21:81 (1986): 55–65, evaluates the efficacy of teaching prosocial problem solving as an alternative to aggression.

Chapter 7: Responses to Anger That Open the Door to Emotional Intimacy

1. Judith Maurin, "Conflict within the Marital Dyad," *Journal of Psychiatric Nursing and Mental Health Services* 12:1 (1974): 31.

2. Ibid., 27–31. This article goes a little further than I do with the idea of reflection as applied to a couple. Maurin discusses how participants in relationships gain self-esteem at the expense of each other. This would lead to greater pathology than what I suggest happens when two identities come together to form a third identity.

3. Judith S. Wallerstein, "The Psychological Tasks of Marriage: Part 2," *American Journal of Orthopsychiatry* 66:2 (1996): 217–27, discusses in depth two tasks of marriage. The couple needs to construct a "safety zone," part of which consists of knowing that the marriage will not end because one person feels angry.

4. Maurin, "Conflict within the Marital Dyad."

5. Wallerstein, "The Psychological Tasks of Marriage: Part 2."

6. Jeffry H. Larson, Clark H. Hammond, and James M. Harper, "Perceived Equity and Intimacy in Marriage," *Journal of Marital and Family Therapy* 24:4 (1998): 487–506, explores the importance of equal partnership in a marriage and the necessity of fairness to achieve that equity.

7. Julia C. Babcock et al., "Power and Violence: The Relation between the Communication Patterns, Power Discrepancies, and Domestic Violence," *Journal of Consulting and Clinical Psychology* 61:1 (1993): 40–50, investigates the importance of communication in maintaining the different power bases of a marriage and the need for equality to arise from those power bases.

8. Annmarie Cano and K. Daniel O'Leary, "Romantic Jealousy and Affairs: Research and Implications for Couple Therapy," *Journal of Sex and Marital Therapy* 23:4 (Winter 1997): 249–75, explores jealousy, response patterns to jealousy, and provides suggestions for changing these patterns.

9. Ibid., 272.

Chapter 8: Positive Responses to Children's Anger

1. Douglas P. Fry, "'Respect for the Rights of Others Is Peace': Learning Aggression versus Nonaggression among the Zapotec," *American Anthropologist* 94 (1992): 621–39, is a fascinating study that investigates in-depth two groups of people from the same heritage, living in different but similar locations in order to answer the question, "What makes them view aggression so differently?"

2. Grace J. Craig, *Human Development,* 7th ed. (Upper Saddle River, N.J.: Prentice-Hall, 1996), gives an exceptional presentation of the various human domains, including the affective, and how they change throughout an individual's life.

3. Edward Z. Tronick, "Emotions and Emotional Communication in Infants," *American Psychologist* 44:2 (1989): 112–19.

4. Cynthia A. Stifter, Tracy L. Spinard, and Julia M. Braungart-Rieker, "Toward a Developmental Model of Child Compliance: The Role of Emotion Regulation in Infancy," *Child Development* 70:1 (1999): 21–32, not only discusses early compliance but examines the importance of self-regulation learned in infancy and its effects on compliance in toddlers.

5. Ibid., 26.

6. Nelson H. Soken and Anne D. Pick, "Infants' Perception of Dynamic Affective Expressions: Do Infants Distinguish Specific Expression?" *Child Development* 70:6 (1999): 1275–82.

7. Tronick, "Emotions and Emotional Communication in Infants," 113.

8. Michael Lewis, "Self-Conscious Emotions," *American Scientist* 83:1 (1995): 68–78, discusses the developmental process of and differences between shame and

guilt, hubris and pride, and shyness and embarrassment. Important to this process is a sense of self because each of these emotions require evaluation of self as either a person or personal behavior.

9. Judy Dunn, Jane Brown, and Lynn Beardsall, "Family Talk about Feeling States and Children's Later Understanding of Other's Emotions," *Developmental Psychology* 27:3 (1991): 448–55, demonstrates the developmental process of feeling states and the individual's ability to empathize with others.

10. Norma Deitch Feshbach, "Learning to Care: A Positive Approach to Child Training and Discipline," *Journal of Clinical Child Psychology* 12:3 (1983): 266–71, presents a number of suggestions on the components of empathy and how to use them to discipline children.

11. Cathy Rindner Tempelsman, "Handling a Biter," *Parents* 70:5 (1995): 50–52, and Alexander K. C. Leung and Joel E. Fagan, "Temper Tantrums," *American Family Physician* 44:2 (1991): 559–63, give specific ideas, along with behavior management approaches, that caretakers can use when dealing with difficult children.

12. Leung and Fagan, "Temper Tantrums."

13. Craig, *Human Development,* 307.

14. John D. Coie et al., "Role of Aggression in Peer Relations: Analysis of Aggression Episodes in Boys' Play Groups," *Child Development* 62:4 (1991): 812–26, indicates that rejection of aggressive boys becomes more prevalent with age.

15. Lisa Ann Boyum and Ross D. Park, "The Role of Family Emotional Expressiveness in the Development of Children's Social Competence," *Journal of Marriage & the Family* 57:3 (1995): 593–608, researches the importance of the emotional atmosphere a young child experiences and its connection to future prosocial behaviors. Jude Cassidy et al., "Family Peer Connections: The Roles of Emotional Expressiveness within the Family and Children's Understanding of Emotions," *Child Development* 63:3 (1992): 603–18, indicates the relationship between parental expressiveness and positive outcomes for children, such as greater emotional expression and better peer relations.

16. Jennifer S. Cummings et al., "Children's Responses to Angry Adult Behavior as a Function of Marital Distress and History of Interparent Hostility," *Child Development* 60:5 (1989): 1035–43.

17. Marion K. Underwood, John D. Coie, and Cheryl R. Herbsman, "Display Rules for Anger and Aggression in School-Aged Children," *Child Development* 63:2 (1992): 366–80.

18. Norma D. Feshbach and Kiki Roe, "Empathy in Six- and Seven-Year-Olds," *Child Development* 39 (1968): 133–45, indicates the difficulty boys have with labeling the sensation of fear. Dayna Fuchs and Mark H. Thelen, "Children's Expected Interpersonal Consequences of Communicating Their Affective State and Reported Likelihood of Expression," *Child Development* 59:5 (1988): 1314–22, finds that boys have difficulty with sadness, as well as with fear.

19. Kenneth A. Dodge and John D. Coie, "Social-Information-Processing Factors in Reactive and Proactive Aggression in Children's Peer Groups," *Journal of Personality and Social Psychology* 53:6 (1987): 1146–58 labels this type of dysfunction as hostile attributional biases and intention-cue detection deficits. Tjeert Olthof, Tamara J. Ferguson, and Annemieke Luiten, "Personal Responsibility Antecedents of Anger and Blame in Children," *Child Development* 60:6 (1989): 1328–36, investigated children's evaluation of events in the context of intentionality and avoidability. When an act was thought to be intentional, the children in the study reacted with anger. But avoidability had a greater impact on their anger reaction. An intentional act, when avoided, tended not to create anger.

20. *CBS News Online*, Reuters (June 3, 2000).

21. John E. Lochman, Susanne E. Dunn, and Bonnie Klimes-Dougan, "An Intervention and Consultation Model from a Social Cognitive Perspective: A Description of the Anger Coping Program," *School Psychology Review* 22:3 (1993): 460.

22. Robert H. DuRant et al., "Weapon Carrying on School Property among Middle School Students," *Archives of Pediatric and Adolescent Medicine* 153 (1999): 22, and Marvin K. Malek, Bei-Hung Chang, and Terry C. Davis, "Fighting and Weapon-Carrying among Seventh Grade Students in Massachusetts and Louisiana," *Journal of Adolescent Health* 23:2 (1998): 98.

23. DuRant, "Weapon Carrying on School Property," 23.

24. Malek, "Fighting and Weapon-Carrying," 99.

25. Ibid.

26. Ibid.

27. Ibid., 98.

28. Mark I. Singer et al., "Viewing Preferences, Symptoms of Psychological Trauma, and Violent Behaviors among Children Who Watch Television," *Journal of American Academy for Child Adolescent Psychiatry* 37:10 (1998): 1041–48, examined two variables with potential relationships to violence and television watching: length of time watched and type of shows watched. The results indicated that violence is not the only potential outcome of excessive (six or more hours per day) television watching. Depression and anxiety were more prevalent among the excessive television viewers.

29. Ibid.

30. Ron Taffel, "Discovering Our Children," *Family Therapy Networker* (September/October 1999): 24–34.

Chapter 9: Effectively Responding to Angry Adolescents

1. Li-yu Song, Mark I. Singer, and Trina M. Anglin, "Violence Exposure and Emotional Trauma as Contributors to Adolescents' Violent Behaviors," *Archives of Pediatric and Adolescent Medicine* 152 (1998): 531–36, discusses a number of studies

that indicate the long-term effects of involvement with violence during childhood. The study, conducted by the article's authors, showed a strong relationship for the students surveyed (mean age of sixteen) between exposure to violence and resultant violent behaviors.

2. Douglas P. Fry, "'Respect for the Rights of Others Is Peace': Learning Aggression versus Nonaggression among the Zapotec," *American Anthropologist* 94 (1992): 621–39.

3. Tony D. Crespi and Sandra A. Rigazio-DiGilio, "Adolescent Homicide and Family Pathology: Implications for Research and Treatment with Adolescents," *Adolescence* 31:122 (1996): 360.

4. Alice J. Hausman, Howard Spivak, and Deborah Prothrow-Stith, "Adolescents' Knowledge and Attitudes about and Experience with Violence," *Journal of Adolescent Health* 15 (1994): 406.

5. Song et al., "Violence Exposure and Emotional Trauma," 536. I have never seen adults defend any issue as rigorously as they do their right to use, and the rightness of using, physical punishment to teach children. I have stopped arguing the point and instead, refer them to the article by Murray A. Straus, "Discipline and Deviance: Physical Punishment of Children and Violence and Other Crime in Adulthood," *Social Problems* 38:2 (May 1991): 133–197. These pages include a discourse on the Straus article by Donileen R. Loseke, "Reply to Murray A. Straus: Readings on 'Discipline and Deviance,'" and a rebuttal by Murray A. Straus, "New Theory and Old Canards about Family Violence Research."

6. Guy S. Diamond and Howard A. Liddle, "Transforming Negative Parent-Adolescent Interactions: From Impasse to Dialogue," *Family Process* 38:1 (1991): 5–25, discusses a similar method of communication that they refer to as "shifting." These authors present examples depicting ways they help, during counseling sessions, parent-adolescent communication impasses by shifting the focus from behavior management problems to the expression of emotions.

Chapter 10: There Is a Time

1. Julia C. Babcock et al., "Power and Violence: The Relation between the Communication Patterns, Power Discrepancies, and Domestic Violence," *Journal of Consulting and Clinical Psychology* 61:1 (1993): 40–50.

Bibliography

Babcock, Julia C., et al. "Power and Violence: The Relation between the Communication Patterns, Power Discrepancies, and Domestic Violence." *Journal of Consulting and Clinical Psychology* 61 (1993): 40–50.

Bandura, Albert. *Aggression: A Social Learning Analysis.* Englewood Cliffs, N.J.: Prentice-Hall, 1973.

Bandura, Albert, Dorothea Ross, and Sheila A. Ross. "Imitation of Film-Mediated Aggressive Models." *Journal of Abnormal and Social Psychology* 66 (1963): 3–11.

Berns, Sara B., Neil S. Jacobson, and John M. Gottman. "Demand/Withdraw Interaction Patterns between Different Types of Batterers and Their Spouses." *Family Therapy* 25 (1999): 337–47.

Boyum, Lisa Ann, and Ross D. Park. "The Role of Family Emotional Expressiveness in the Development of Children's Social Competence." *Journal of Marriage & the Family* 57 (1995): 593–608.

Cano, Annmarie, and K. Daniel O'Leary. "Romantic Jealousy and Affairs: Research and Implications for Couple Therapy." *Journal of Sex and Marital Therapy* 23 (Winter 1997): 249–75.

Cassidy, Jude, et al. "Family Peer Connections: The Roles of Emotional Expressiveness within the Family and Children's Understanding of Emotions." *Child Development* 63 (1992): 603–18.

Coie, John D., et al. "Role of Aggression in Peer Relations: Analysis of Aggression Episodes in Boys' Play Groups." *Child Development* 62 (1991): 812–26.

Craig, Grace J. *Human Development,* 7th ed. Upper Saddle River, N.J.: Prentice-Hall, 1996.

Crespi, Tony D., and Sandra A. Rigazio-DiGilio. "Adolescent Homicide and Family Pathology: Implications for Research and Treatment with Adolescents." *Adolescence* 31 (1996): 353–65.

Cummings, Jennifer S., et al. "Children's Responses to Angry Adult Behavior as a Function of Marital Distress and History of Interparent Hostility." *Child Development* 60 (1989): 1035–43.

Diamond, Guy S., and Howard A. Liddle. "Transforming Negative Parent-Adolescent Interactions: From Impasse to Dialogue." *Family Process* 38 (1991): 5–25.

Dodge, Kenneth A., and John D. Coie. "Social-Information-Processing Factors in Reactive and Proactive Aggression in Children's Peer Groups." *Journal of Personality and Social Psychology* 53 (1987): 1146–58.

Dodge, Kenneth A., and Nicki R. Crick. "Social Information-Processing Bases of Aggressive Behavior in Children." *Personality and Social Psychology* 16 (1990): 8–22.

Dunn, Judy, Jane Brown, and Lynn Beardsall. "Family Talk about Feeling States and Children's Later Understanding of Other's Emotions." *Developmental Psychology* 27 (1991): 448–55.

DuRant, Robert H., et al. "Weapon Carrying on School Property among Middle School Students." *Archives of Pediatric and Adolescent Medicine* 153 (1999): 21–26.

Feshbach, Norma D., and Kiki Roe. "Empathy in Six- and Seven-Year-Olds." *Child Development* 39 (1968): 133–45.

Feshbach, Norma Deitch. "Learning to Care: A Positive Approach to Child Training and Discipline." *Journal of Clinical Child Psychology* 12 (1983): 266–71.

Fidler, Eric. "Antisocial Behavior in Boys Studied." Associated Press (January 13, 2000).

Fritzlan, Larry. "Raising the Bottom: Setting Limits for Teenage Substance Abusers." *Networker* (July/August 1999): 61–64.

Fry, Douglas P. "'Respect for the Rights of Others Is Peace': Learning Aggression versus Nonaggression among the Zapotec." *American Anthropologist* 94 (1992): 621–39.

Fuchs, Dayna, and Mark H. Thelen. "Children's Expected Interpersonal Consequences of Communicating Their Affective State and Reported Likelihood of Expression." *Child Development* 59 (1988): 1314–22.

Goodwin, Megan P., and Bruce Roscoe. "Sibling Violence and Agonistic Interactions among Middle Adolescents." *Adolescence* 25 (1990): 451–67.

Hausman, Alice J., Howard Spivak, and Deborah Prothrow-Stith. "Adolescents' Knowledge and Attitudes about and Experience with Violence." *Journal of Adolescent Health* 15 (1994): 400–06.

Hornstein, Harvey A. *Cruelty and Kindness: A New Look at Aggression and Altruism.* Englewood Cliffs, N.J.: Prentice-Hall, 1976.

Jacobson, Edmund. *Biology of Emotions.* Springfield, Ill.: Charles C. Thomas, 1967.

Jamison, Robert N., E. Warren Lambert, and Danny J. McCloud. "Social Skills Training with Hospitalized Adolescents: An Evaluative Experiment." *Adolescence* 21 (1986): 55–65.

Larson, Jeffry H., Clark H. Hammond, and James M. Harper. "Perceived Equity and Intimacy in Marriage." *Journal of Marital and Family Therapy* 24 (1998): 487–506.

Leung, Alexander K. C., and Joel E. Fagan. "Temper Tantrums." *American Family Physician* 44 (1991): 559–63.

Lewis, Michael. "Self-Conscious Emotions." *American Scientist* 83 (1995): 68–78.

Lochman, John E., Susanne E. Dunn, and Bonnie Klimes-Dougan. "An Intervention and Consultation Model from a Social Cognitive Perspective: A Description of the Anger Coping Program." *School Psychology Review* 22 (1993): 458–71.

Malek, Marvin K., Bei-Hung Chang, and Terry C. Davis. "Fighting and Weapon-Carrying among Seventh Grade Students in Massachusetts and Louisiana." *Journal of Adolescent Health* 23 (1998): 94–102.

Marshall, John R. "The Expression of Feelings." *Archives of General Psychiatry* 27 (1972): 786–90.

Maurin, Judith. "Conflict within the Marital Dyad." *Journal of Psychiatric Nursing and Mental Health Services* 12 (1974): 27–31.

Minde, Klaus. "Aggression in Preschoolers: Its Relation to Socialization." *Journal of American Academy of Child and Adolescent Psychiatry* 31 (1992): 853–62.

Novaco, Raymond W. "Stress Inoculation: A Cognitive Therapy for Anger and Its Application to a Case of Depression." *Journal of Consulting and Clinical Psychology* 47 (1977): 600–08.

Olthof, Tjeert, Tamara J. Ferguson, and Annemieke Luiten. "Personal Responsibility Antecedents of Anger and Blame in Children." *Child Development* 60 (1989): 1328–36.

Prinz, Ronald J., Elaine A. Blechman, and Jean E. Dumas. "An Evaluation of Peer Coping Skills Training for Childhood Aggression." *Journal of Clinical Child Psychology* 23 (1994): 193–203.

Scarpa, Angela, and Adrian Raine. "Psychophysiology of Anger and Violent Behavior." *The Psychiatric Clinics of North America* 20 (1997): 375–94.

Siegman, Aron W. "Cardiovascular Consequences of Expressing, Experiencing, and Repressing Anger." *Journal of Behavioral Medicine* 16 (1993): 539–69.

Singer, Mark I., et al. "Contributors to Violent Behavior among Elementary and Middle School Children." *Pediatrics* 104 (1999): 878–84.

Singer, Mark I., et al. "Viewing Preferences, Symptoms of Psychological Trauma, and Violent Behaviors among Children Who Watch Television." *Journal of American Academy for Child Adolescent Psychiatry* 37 (1998): 1041–48.

Soken, Nelson H., and Anne D. Pick. "Infants' Perception of Dynamic Affective Expressions: Do Infants Distinguish Specific Expression?" *Child Development* 70 (1999): 1275–82.

Song, Li-yu, Mark I. Singer, and Trina M. Anglin. "Violence Exposure and Emotional Trauma as Contributors to Adolescents' Violent Behaviors." *Archives of Pediatric and Adolescent Medicine* 152 (1998): 531–36.

Stifter, Cynthia A., Tracy L. Spinard, and Julia M. Braungart-Rieker. "Toward a Developmental Model of Child Compliance: The Role of Emotion Regulation in Infancy." *Child Development* 70 (1999): 21–32.

Straus, Murray A. "Discipline and Deviance: Physical Punishment of Children and Violence and Other Crime in Adulthood." *Social Problems* 38 (May 1991): 133–197.

Taffel, Ron. "Discovering Our Children." *Family Therapy Networker* (September/October 1999): 24–34.

Tavris, Carol. *Anger: The Misunderstood Emotion.* New York: Simon & Schuster, 1982.

Tempelsman, Cathy Rindner. "Handling a Biter." *Parents* 70 (1995): 50–52.

Tronick, Edward Z. "Emotions and Emotional Communication in Infants." *American Psychologist* 44 (1989): 112–19.

Underwood, Marion K., John D. Coie, and Cheryl R. Herbsman. "Display Rules for Anger and Aggression in School-Aged Children." *Child Development* 63 (1992): 366–80.

Wallerstein, Judith S. "The Psychological Tasks of Marriage: Part 2." *American Journal of Orthopsychiatry* 66 (1996): 217–27.

Weis, Bahr, et al. "Some Consequences of Early Harsh Discipline: Child Aggression and a Maladaptive Social Information Processing Style." *Child Development* 63 (1992): 1321–35.

About the Author

Lorrainne Bilodeau, M.S., is a certified addictions counselor and program director of treatment facilities. She is the author of *The Anger Workbook* and has directed workshops and seminars that teach people throughout the country to express and respond to anger in healthy ways.